SpringerBriefs in Criminology

More information about this series at http://www.springer.com/series/10159

AF793665

Wesley G. Jennings • Rolf Loeber
Dustin A. Pardini • Alex R. Piquero
David P. Farrington

Offending from Childhood to Young Adulthood

Recent Results from the Pittsburgh Youth Study

Springer

Wesley G. Jennings
Department of Criminology
University of South Florida
Tampa, FL, USA

Dustin A. Pardini
School of Criminology and Criminal Justice
Arizona State University
Phoenix, AZ, USA

Rolf Loeber
Department of Psychiatry
University of Pittsburgh
Pittsburgh, PA, USA

David P. Farrington
Institute of Criminology
Cambridge University
UK

Alex R. Piquero
School of Economic, Political,
and Policy Sciences
University of Texas at Dallas
Richardson, Texas, USA

ISSN 2192-8533 ISSN 2192-8541 (electronic)
SpringerBriefs in Criminology
ISBN 978-3-319-25965-9 ISBN 978-3-319-25966-6 (eBook)
DOI 10.1007/978-3-319-25966-6

Library of Congress Control Number: 2015959270

Springer Cham Heidelberg New York Dordrecht London
© The Authors 2016
This work is subject to copyright. All rights are reserved by the Publisher, whether the whole or part of the material is concerned, specifically the rights of translation, reprinting, reuse of illustrations, recitation, broadcasting, reproduction on microfilms or in any other physical way, and transmission or information storage and retrieval, electronic adaptation, computer software, or by similar or dissimilar methodology now known or hereafter developed.
The use of general descriptive names, registered names, trademarks, service marks, etc. in this publication does not imply, even in the absence of a specific statement, that such names are exempt from the relevant protective laws and regulations and therefore free for general use.
The publisher, the authors and the editors are safe to assume that the advice and information in this book are believed to be true and accurate at the date of publication. Neither the publisher nor the authors or the editors give a warranty, express or implied, with respect to the material contained herein or for any errors or omissions that may have been made.

Printed on acid-free paper

Springer International Publishing AG Switzerland is part of Springer Science+Business Media (www.springer.com)

Acknowledgments

The authors are greatly indebted to the staff of the Pittsburgh Youth Study, especially Magda Stouthamer-Loeber. Rebecca Stalling effectively assembled the data for analyses, while Jennifer Wilson kindly checked the references. The research on which this book is based was funded by grants from the National Institute of Mental Health (MH056630, MH 48890, MH 50778), the Office of Juvenile Justice and Delinquency Prevention (2013-JF-FX-0058), the National Institute on Drug Abuse (DA411018), Pew Charitable Trusts, Office of Juvenile Justice and Delinquency Prevention (96-MU-FX-0012), and the Pennsylvania Department of Health (SAP 4100043365).

Acknowledgments

Contents

About the Authors

Wesley G. Jennings, Ph.D. is Associate Professor, Associate Chair, and Undergraduate Director in the Department of Criminology, has a Courtesy Appointment in the Department of Mental Health Law and Policy, and is a Faculty Affiliate of the Florida Mental Health Institute in the College of Behavioral and Community Sciences at the University of South Florida. In addition, he also has a Courtesy Appointment in the Department of Health Outcomes and Policy and is a Faculty Affiliate of the Institute for Child Health Policy in the College of Medicine at the University of Florida. He received his doctorate degree in criminology from the University of Florida. He has nearly 200 publications, his *h*-index is 28 (*i*-index of 72), and he has nearly 3,000 citations to his published work. He was recently recognized as the #1 criminologist in the world (at his previous rank of Assistant Professor: Copes et al., *JCJE*, 2013) and the #3 criminologist in the world *across all ranks* in terms of his peer-reviewed scholarly publication productivity in the top criminology and criminal justice journals (Cohn and Farrington, *JCJE*, 2014). He is also the author (with David Farrington and Alex Piquero) of a recently published, academic press book with Springer, *Offending from Childhood to Late Middle Age: Recent Results from the Cambridge Study in Delinquent Development*, and is the author (with Jennifer Reingle) of a recently published textbook with Wolters Kluwer, *Criminological and Criminal Justice Research Methods*.

Rolf Loeber, Ph.D. is Distinguished University Professor of Psychiatry and Professor of Psychology and Epidemiology at the University of Pittsburgh, Pittsburgh, Pennsylvania. He is the Director of the Life History Program and is the initiator of two large longitudinal studies, the Pittsburgh Youth Study and the Pittsburgh Girls Study. He has published widely in the fields of juvenile antisocial behavior and delinquency, substance use, and mental health problems. He is an Elected Member of the Koninklijke Academie van Wetenschappen (Royal Academy of Sciences) in the Netherlands and the Royal Irish Academy in Ireland.

Dustin A. Pardini, Ph.D. is an Associate Professor in the School of Criminology and Criminal Justice at Arizona State University. He originally began working with

Drs. Rolf Loeber and Magda Stouthamer-Loeber as a Postdoctoral Fellow on the Pittsburgh Youth Study at the University of Pittsburgh in 2003, becoming Codirector of the study in 2011. He has comanaged the last three longitudinal follow-ups of the PYS participants and led efforts to update the official criminal record database to include offenses that occurred from 2000 to 2011. He is currently involved with four grants as Principal Investigator and one as Coinvestigator to continue data collection, analysis, and archiving activities with the PYS samples.

Alex R. Piquero, Ph.D. is the Ashbel Smith Professor of Criminology and Associate Dean for Graduate Programs in the School of Economic, Political, and Policy Sciences at the University of Texas at Dallas and Adjunct Professor with the Key Centre for Ethics, Law, Justice, and Governance at Griffith University. From 2008 until 2013, he was Coeditor of the *Journal of Quantitative Criminology*. He has published over 300 peer-reviewed articles in the areas of criminal careers, criminological theory, and quantitative research methods and has collaborated on several books including *Key Issues in Criminal Careers Research*: *New Analyses from the Cambridge Study in Delinquent Development* (coauthored with David P. Farrington and Alfred Blumstein) and *Handbook of Quantitative Criminology* (coedited by David Weisburd). In addition to his membership on over a dozen editorial boards of journals in criminology and sociology, he has also served as Executive Counselor with the American Society of Criminology; Member of the National Academy of Sciences Panel Evaluating the National Institute of Justice; Member of the National Academy of Sciences Panel on Modernizing Crime Statistics; Member of the National Academy of Sciences Panel on a Prioritized Plan to Implement a Developmental Approach in Juvenile Justice Reform; Member of the Racial Democracy, Crime and Justice Network at Ohio State University; and Member of the MacArthur Foundation's Research Network on Adolescent Development & Juvenile Justice. He is also Fellow of both the American Society of Criminology and the Academy of Criminal Justice Sciences, and in 2014 he received the University of Texas System Regents' Outstanding Teaching Award. Dr. Piquero received his Ph.D. in criminology and criminal justice from the University of Maryland at College Park.

David P. Farrington is Emeritus Professor of Psychological Criminology in the Institute of Criminology, Cambridge University. He received the Stockholm Prize in criminology in 2013. He is Chair of the American Society of Criminology Division of Developmental and Life-Course Criminology. His major research interest is in developmental criminology, and he is a Director of the Cambridge Study in Delinquent Development, a prospective longitudinal survey of over 400 London males from age 8 to age 56. In addition to over 650 published journal articles and book chapters on criminological and psychological topics, he has published nearly 100 books, monographs, and government reports.

Chapter 1
Introduction to Criminal Careers

Nearly 100 years following Adolphe Quetelet's classic (1831) *Research on the Propensity for Crime at Different Ages*, Clifford Shaw (1930) delivered his seminal and qualitative criminal career study of a delinquent youth named Stanley in the *Jack Roller*. Coinciding during this same era, Sheldon and Eleanor Glueck (1950; 1968) can be credited with ushering in the beginning of in-depth quantitative criminal career research with their detailed examination of delinquents and non-delinquents and identifying correlates of offending over the life-course. Soon thereafter, Wolfgang et al. (1972) embarked on one of the most well-known and comprehensive, life-course offending, cohort-based studies, commonly referred to as the Philadelphia Birth Cohort Study, with their initial findings published in *Delinquency in a Birth Cohort*.

Since these early works, there have been a host of very well-respected, longitudinal, and/or birth cohort studies in criminology. A brief list of some of these study sites with the central affiliated authors includes: Second Philadelphia Birth Cohort (Tracy), Seattle (Hawkins and Catalano), Racine, Wisconsin (Shannon), London (West and Farrington), Montreal (Le Blanc and Tremblay), Dunedin (Moffitt), and Christchurch (Fergusson), and three interrelated studies funded by the Office of Juvenile Justice and Delinquency Prevention in Denver, Rochester, and Pittsburgh (Huizinga, Thornberry, Loeber). Although much more detailed reviews of criminal career research can be found elsewhere (Blumstein et al. 1986; Piquero et al. 2003, 2007, 2012), it is important to highlight some of the key findings that have emerged from these studies and this literature on the most noted of the criminal career dimensions that are relevant for this book: prevalence, frequency, onset, and criminal career duration. For example, regarding the prevalence of offending, in official records, estimates range from about one-third to almost one-half, experiencing either a police contact, arrest, or conviction depending on the data source and length of follow-up (see Blumstein et al. 1986; Brame et al. 2012). With self-report records, Farrington (2002) has reported that 96 % of the males from the Cambridge Study in Delinquent Development (CSDD) had self-reported some form of offending by age 32, and nearly two out of every five of the males had been convicted at least once by age 30.

© The Authors 2016

W.G. Jennings et al., *Offending from Childhood to Young Adulthood*,
SpringerBriefs in Criminology, DOI 10.1007/978-3-319-25966-6_1

Similarly, Moffitt et al. (2001) reported that 91 % of the males and 86 % of the females in the Dunedin Health and Human Development Study had engaged in delinquent activity by age 18.

Concerning the frequency of offending, Piquero et al.'s (2003) comprehensive review of criminal career research investigating lambda (λ) found that self-reported offense frequency generally peaked in mid-adolescence (age 16) before declining slowly thereafter into young adulthood. In contrast, official offending tended to peak at ages 17–20, which is likely due in part to differences between the juvenile and adult justice system in terms of consistency in recording records, police not officially charging juveniles, etc. In addition, Spelman (1994) has reported that in the Rand Inmate Survey, the average offender commits approximately eight crimes per year when they are actively offending, and among those with prior incarceration experiences, this annual rate of offending can be estimated to be as high as 30–50 crimes per year. Farrington et al. (1998, 2013) have also reported a high level of continuity in offending over time, particularly for those with a higher level of offending frequency.

Age of onset and criminal career length are two related criminal career concepts, with the former referring to the age at which the first offense is committed and the latter referring to the duration between onset age (e.g., age at first offense) and age at last offense. Generally speaking, most studies report the age of onset as being between ages 13 and 19 (Elliott et al. 1987; Tibbetts and Piquero 1999), although studies have noted that it is generally earlier in self-reports and later in official records (see Moffitt et al. 2001) and also that onset age varies by crime type. For example, Farrington (1990) reported an onset age of 13–14 for shoplifting and 17–19 for assault. Nevertheless, it is a well-known fact in the criminal career literature that an earlier onset predicts a longer and more frequent criminal career (Farrington et al. 1998; Fabio et al. 2006; Piquero et al. 2012). For example, Piquero et al. (2003, 2007) demonstrated that two-thirds of the offenders who were active at ages 10–15 were also still active at ages 16–20, whereas those offenders whose onset age was later (ages 21–30) committed fewer offenses overall and had shorter criminal careers of 2.3 years. Furthermore, Farrington (1992) indicated an average criminal career length of 10.4 years when looking only at those offenders who committed more than one offense over their life-course. Lengthier criminal career estimates have also been reported in the literature. For instance, relying on a sample of California Youth Authority parolees, Piquero et al. (2004) observed an average criminal career length of 17.3 years, and Laub and Sampson (2003) reported an average criminal career length among the Gluecks' delinquents of 25.6 years when followed through age 70, but there was substantial variation among delinquents. Ultimately, in order to obtain an accurate estimate of the age of desistance and criminal career length, it is important to follow up offenders beyond age 40 if possible.

With this criminal career research and developmental/life-course literature as a framework, this book is designed to offer the most extensive and comprehensive investigation to date on the official offending, self-reported offending, and trajectories of offending of the Pittsburgh Youth Study (PYS) participants. Specifically, the PYS is a longitudinal study, which was initiated in 1987, and involves repeated follow-ups on several community cohorts of inner-city boys in Pittsburgh, Pennsylvania. When first contacted for participation, the boys were in grades 1, 4, and 7 in Pittsburgh's public schools and are commonly referred to as the Youngest, Middle, and Oldest cohorts, respectively. Consistent with several prior publications with the PYS data (Loeber et al. 2008), this book focuses only on data from the Youngest and Oldest cohorts as these cohorts were followed up the most frequently and have the longest time window of data available.

For these particular cohorts, comprehensive public school lists were obtained for the 1631 and 1419 male students who were enrolled in grades 1 and 7, respectively. From these targeted lists, approximately 1100 boys in each of the grades were randomly selected to be contacted. Following the filtering out of boys who had moved out of the school district, the girls, and the boys who were of an incorrect age, a total of 1004 families of boys in grade 1 and 1020 families of boys in grade 7 were contacted. The final sample sizes (N) for the Youngest and Oldest Cohorts were 503 and 506, respectively. Overall, the participation rate of the boys and their parents were 84.6 % and 83.9 % for the Youngest and Oldest cohorts, respectively. Details about the individual assessment of the young males in the two cohorts at successive assessments can be found in Chap. 3 (especially Table 3.1), and a complete list of previous PYS publications are listed in Appendix 1.

The chapters that follow detail the official offending, self-reported offending, and trajectories of offending for the Youngest and Oldest PYS cohorts from ages 10–30 and, as such, provide the most complete descriptive analyses of the criminal careers of these males to date. To some extent, this book complements the earlier Springer Brief by Farrington et al. (2013), which details many of these topics for the Cambridge Study in Delinquent Development (CSDD). In the concluding Chap. 5, we will compare the results from the CSDD and the PYS. The fundamental information presented in this book about offending needs to be considered in criminological theories and policies.

Chapter 2
Official Criminal Careers

2.1 Measurement of Official Offending in the PYS

Juvenile court conviction data was obtained from the Allegheny County Juvenile Court Records for offenses that occurred within Allegheny County (ages 10–18), and the Pennsylvania Juvenile Court Judges' Commission provided juvenile conviction data for offenses that occurred throughout the state of Pennsylvania. Comparatively, adult conviction data was obtained from the Pennsylvania State Police Repository and The Unified Judicial System of Pennsylvania Web Portal (https://ujsportal.pacourts.us) for offenses that were committed in the state of Pennsylvania and the Federal Bureau of Investigation (FBI) for offenses committed outside of Pennsylvania for the PYS participants. Loeber et al. (2008) reported that the Allegheny County Juvenile Court records were searched and coded for offense date, offense category, and disposition and that an official record project initiative was undertaken to integrate all of the conviction data from the youths' court records from the Allegheny County Juvenile Court, the Commonwealth of Pennsylvania, and the FBI. All data was initially double entered, and discrepancies were corrected. Identical criminal cases across sources were matched using their assigned Offense Tracking Number, a unique number given out by the court system to every criminal case upon processing of a criminal complaint. Discrepancies across multiple sources were reviewed to avoid double counting charges and to ensure that all relevant charges and dispositions were included in the final dataset.

Following this integration, all complete data on the number of *conviction charges* (e.g., the crime-specific charges that the participant was convicted for) were coded based on the definition of the crimes in the FBI's Uniform Crime Reports.[1] This coding scheme is consistent with that used by the National Center for Juvenile Justice (Homish 2002). For analytic purposes and to enable direct comparisons with

[1] Additionally, it is important to note that these offenses are based on conviction charges. As such, one criminal event could result in multiple convictions.

© The Authors 2016

W.G. Jennings et al., *Offending from Childhood to Young Adulthood*, SpringerBriefs in Criminology, DOI 10.1007/978-3-319-25966-6_2

Table 2.1 Prevalence of official offenders: Youngest and Oldest cohorts (TOTAL SAMPLE)

	Percent at age				All ages
Offense type	10–14	15–18	19–24	25–30	
Youngest cohort					
Moderate theft	6.4	13.1	10.3	5.6	24.6
Serious theft	4.2	6.4	5.1	2.3	13.0
Moderate violence	4.4	6.0	8.1	5.8	19.8
Serious violence	7.2	8.8	7.7	3.3	20.7
Drug dealing	0.6	4.8	11.3	6.0	16.5
Any theft, violence, or drug dealing	14.5	24.4	26.5	16.7	42.4
Oldest cohort					
Moderate theft	9.3	22.1	9.7	4.7	32.9
Serious theft	8.3	16.2	5.9	1.2	22.4
Moderate violence	2.2	9.3	9.3	4.7	19.9
Serious violence	3.6	10.1	9.1	4.1	20.3
Drug dealing	0.0	5.5	13.2	7.8	20.7
Any theft, violence, or drug dealing	14.6	34.0	31.4	16.0	50.1

the self-report PYS data, the official conviction charges data relied on here are comprised of five crime types that have been utilized frequently in the literature when using data from the PYS (see Loeber et al. 2008). Specifically, *moderate theft* is defined as larceny or dealing in stolen property; *serious theft* is burglary or motor vehicle theft; *moderate violence* is simple assault; *serious violence* is defined as robbery, homicide, voluntary manslaughter, rape, aggravated assault, involuntary deviate sexual intercourse, aggravated indecent assault, or spousal sexual assault; and *drug dealing* is the selling of marijuana or hard drugs.[2]

2.2 Prevalence of Official Offending

Table 2.1 displays the prevalence of official conviction charges in the PYS for the Youngest and Oldest cohorts by age bands (i.e., ages 10–14, ages 15–18, ages 19–24, and ages 25–30) and by crime type (e.g., moderate theft, serious theft, moderate violence, serious violence, and drug dealing) as well as overall prevalence estimates. Approximately, 6.4 % of the Youngest cohort had convictions for moderate theft, 4.2 % for serious theft, 4.4 % for moderate violence, 7.2 % for serious violence, and 0.6 % for drug dealing at ages 10–14. In comparison, the following prevalence estimates were observed for the Oldest Cohort at ages 10–14: moderate theft (9.3 %), serious theft (8.3 %), moderate violence (2.2 %), serious violence (3.6 %), and drug dealing (0.0 %). Drug dealing became the most prevalent offense at ages 19–24 for

[2]Although arrest data also exists in the PYS, we relied on conviction data to measure official offending in order to be consistent with Farrington et al.'s (2013) recent life-course investigation of a similarly lengthy follow-up of a prospective longitudinal sample using data from the Cambridge Study in Delinquent Development.

both the Youngest cohort (11.3 %) and the Oldest cohort (13.2 %). Finally, the overall prevalence for any crime at any age band was 42.4 %, and the age band-specific prevalence estimates were as follows for the Youngest cohort: 14.5 % (ages 10–14), 24.4 % (ages 15–18), 26.5 % (ages 19–24), and 16.7 % (ages 25–30). In contrast, approximately, one half of the Oldest cohort were convicted at some point for some type of crime, with age band-specific prevalence estimates being 14.6 % (ages 10–14), 34.0 % (ages 15–18), 31.4 % (ages 19–24), and 16.0 % (ages 25–30).

2.3 Age and Crime

With regard to the relationship between age and officially recorded crime in the PYS, Table 2.2 reports the number of active offenders and their total number of offenses at each individual age from ages 10 to 30 for the Youngest cohort. As can be seen, there were only a handful of active offenders at ages 10 and 11, mainly having one offense each. The number of active offenders then precipitously increased

Table 2.2 Changes in official offending with age: Youngest cohort (ACTIVE OFFENDERS)

Age	No. of offenders	% of cohort	No. of offenses	Mean no. of offenses	Range of offenses
10	2	1.0	2	0.01	0–1
11	4	2.0	7	0.03	0–3
12	15	6.3	23	0.10	0–3
13	26	12.2	56	0.26	0–7
14	45	20.5	84	0.38	0–4
15	42	20.0	106	0.51	0–17
16	49	22.0	108	0.50	0–11
17	36	16.1	60	0.28	0–4
18	49	22.9	115	0.53	0–11
19	54	25.9	115	0.55	0–11
20	33	15.1	67	0.30	0–7
21	33	15.6	61	0.29	0–11
22	34	16.6	59	0.29	0–9
23	22	10.2	40	0.19	0–6
24	28	13.2	44	0.21	0–4
25	19	8.8	30	0.14	0–5
26	18	8.8	26	0.13	0–4
27	22	10.7	45	0.22	0–8
28	15	7.3	23	0.11	0–3
29	21	10.2	38	0.19	0–7
30	10	4.9	11	0.05	0–2
Total	205	100.0	1080	5.27	0–33

Note: Column does not sum to 1080 as the sample size varies in terms of the number of males at risk over age due to participant mortality.

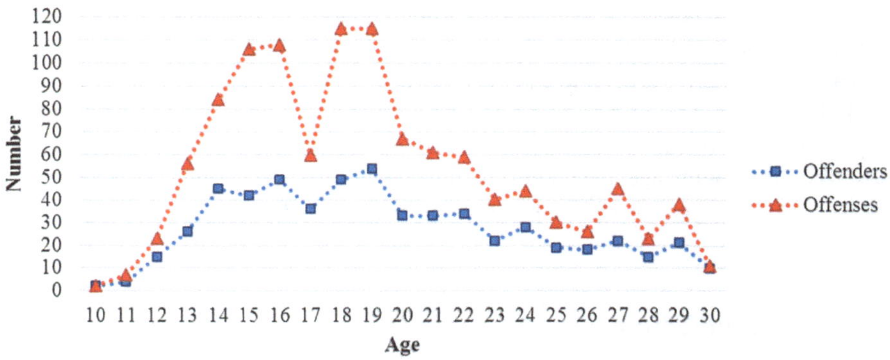

Fig. 2.1 Distribution of the number of offenses and offenders across ages 10–30: Youngest cohort (ACTIVE OFFENDERS)

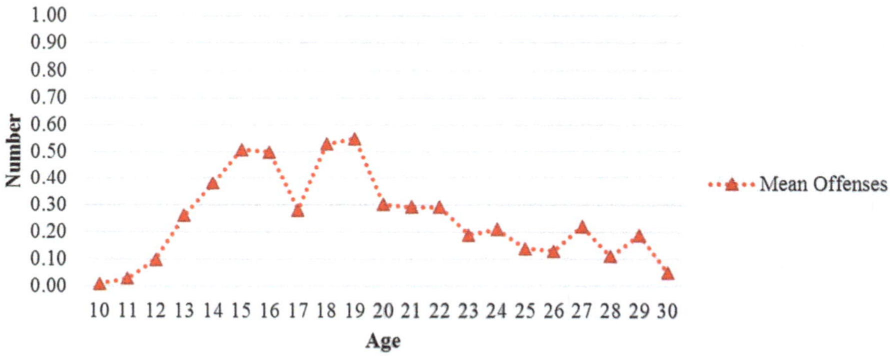

Fig. 2.2 Distribution of the mean (average) number of offenses across ages 10–30: Youngest cohort (ACTIVE OFFENDERS)

throughout adolescence, peaking at age 19 in terms of the number of active offenders (54 offenders) and at ages 18 and 19 in terms of the total number of offenses (115 offenses). Subsequently, the number of active offenders declined in the 20s before reaching a low point in this time period at age 30 (10 offenders; 11 offenses). Overall, for the Youngest cohort, there were 205 participants who were convicted at some point in ages 10–30, and these convicted participants accumulated 1080 offenses over this time period (an average of five offenses each). Figure 2.1 presents a graphical display of the age-crime curve for the Youngest cohort by number of active offenders and number of offenses over age, and Fig. 2.2 presents the age-crime curve by mean (average) number of offenses committed by age.

Table 2.3 provides this similar age-crime breakdown for the Oldest cohort. Specifically, very few participants had offenses at ages 10 and 11, and the number of active offenders increased during adolescence before peaking at age 16 in terms of active offenders (76 offenders) and at age 15 in terms of the total number of offenses committed (210 offenses). In young adulthood, the number of active

Table 2.3 Changes in official offending with age: Oldest cohort (ACTIVE OFFENDERS)

Age	No. of offenders	% of cohort	No. of offenses	Mean no. of offenses	Range of offenses
10	1	<1.0	1	<0.01	0–1
11	1	<1.0	1	<0.01	0–1
12	10	3.7	16	0.06	0–4
13	26	9.4	55	0.21	0–6
14	52	19.7	146	0.55	0–13
15	72	26.2	210	0.79	0–18
16	76	29.5	201	0.77	0–23
17	61	22.5	152	0.59	0–24
18	59	23.4	128	0.51	0–7
19	56	20.9	114	0.44	0–7
20	46	17.2	90	0.34	0–7
21	32	12.3	70	0.28	0–7
22	27	10.7	45	0.18	0–7
23	36	14.8	55	0.23	0–5
24	30	12.3	56	0.23	0–7
25	20	8.8	32	0.12	0–3
26	13	5.3	16	0.07	0–2
27	24	9.8	53	0.22	0–12
28	19	8.8	35	0.14	0–5
29	12	4.9	18	0.07	0–3
30	12	4.9	21	0.09	0–9
Total	244	100.0	1437	5.89	0–42

Note: Column does not sum to 1437 as the sample size varies in terms of the number of males at risk due to participant mortality.

offenders ranged from a low of 12 (age 29 and age 30) to a high of 56 (age 19) with a range of 18 (age 29) to 114 (age 19) offenses. Overall, 244 Oldest cohort participants were convicted at some point at ages 10–30, and these convicted members amassed 1437 offenses over this time period. The age-crime curve by number of active offenders and number of convictions over age for the Oldest cohort is illustrated in Fig. 2.3, and Fig. 2.4 presents the age-crime curve by mean (average) number of offenses committed by age.[3]

[3] It is necessary to point out here that our analyses in this book are all presented separately for the Youngest and Oldest PYS cohorts in order to be consistent with prior PYS studies and analysis (e.g., see Loeber et al. 2008) and due to prior PYS research that has reported period effects. Specifically, Fabio et al. (2006) evaluated the potential influence of age, period, and cohort effects on violence for the Youngest and Oldest PYS cohorts. Their analyses revealed that the Oldest cohort reported higher levels of violence even after accounting for age and a host of individual-level and community-level risk factors. Interestingly, once period effects were introduced into the equation, the cohort effects were no longer observed. These results led the authors to conclude that the differences in offending that were observed (e.g., the higher rates of offending among the

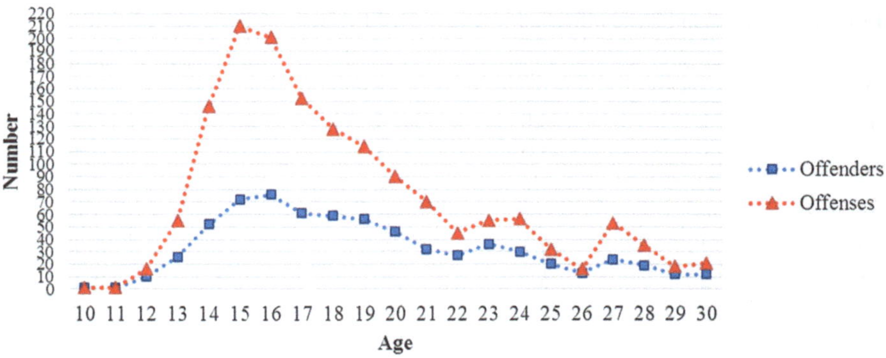

Fig. 2.3 Distribution of the number of offenses and offenders across ages 10–30: Oldest cohort (ACTIVE OFFENDERS)

Fig. 2.4 Distribution of the mean (average) number of offenses across ages 10–30: Oldest cohort (ACTIVE OFFENDERS)

2.4 Continuity in Official Offending

As reported in Table 2.4, the Odds Ratios indicate a significant degree of continuity in offending over the various age bands. For instance, among the Youngest cohort participants who were convicted at ages 10–14, 62.0 % were convicted at ages 15–18, 67.6 % were convicted at ages 19–24, and 42.6 % were convicted at ages 25–30. The corresponding Odds Ratios for these age band comparisons were all statistically significant and ranged from 3.5 to 8.5. Comparatively, nearly three-fourths (73.0 %) of the Oldest cohort who were convicted at ages 10–14 were also

Oldest PYS cohort) were likely attributable to social factors or period effects (such as growing up during the crack epidemic and in a time when crime rates were high in general and in the inner cities specifically) and not necessarily due to cohort effects or differences between the individuals in the Youngest and Oldest PYS cohorts. Therefore, cohort differences in offending that are documented in this book and analyses should be interpreted with recognition of the previously documented existence of and reasons for period effects.

Table 2.4 Continuity in official offending: Youngest and Oldest cohorts (ACTIVE OFFENDERS and NON-OFFENDERS)

Age 1	Age 2	Age 1 and Age 2	Age 2 and not Age 1	OR
Youngest cohort				
10–14	15–18	62.0 % (n=78)	18.2 % (n=44)	7.3
10–14	19–24	67.6 % (n=48)	19.6 % (n=83)	8.5
10–14	25–30	42.6 % (n=29)	12.5 % (n=52)	5.2
15–18	19–24	60.7 % (n=71)	15.9 % (n=60)	8.2
15–18	25–30	35.7 % (n=41)	10.8 % (n=40)	4.6
19–24	25–30	31.5 % (n=40)	11.5 % (n=41)	3.5
Oldest cohort				
10–14	15–18	73.0 % (n=54)	27.3 % (n=118)	7.2
10–14	19–24	66.7 % (n=46)	25.7 % (n=109)	7.0
10–14	25–30	44.1 % (n=30)	11.5 % (n=48)	6.1
15–18	19–24	55.2 % (n=90)	19.7 % (n=65)	5.0
15–18	25–30	30.0 % (n=48)	9.2 % (n=30)	4.2
19–24	25–30	32.9 % (n=50)	8.4 % (n=28)	5.4

Note: Age 1 and Age 2 = percentage of those who offended at age 1, who also offended at age 2; Age 2 and not Age 1 = percentage of those who did not offend at age 1, but who offended at Age 2; OR = Odds Ratio (all ORs are statistically significant, $p<0.05$, one tailed).

convicted at ages 15–18, approximately two-thirds (66.7 %) of the Oldest cohort convicted at ages 10–14 were also convicted at ages 19–24, and 44.1 % of the Oldest cohort convicted at ages 10–14 were also convicted at ages 25–30. The corresponding Odds Ratios for these age band comparisons, all of which were statistically significant as well, ranged from 4.2 to 7.2.

2.5 Criminal Careers

There are many additional dimensions germane to criminal careers, and we further focus here on participation, frequency (e.g., total number of offenses not offending rate per year), age of onset, age of the last offense, and career length. With regard to participation and frequency, Table 2.5 reveals the number of the Youngest cohort participants that were convicted and not convicted between ages 10 and 30, the cumulative percentage of participants by the number of offenses committed, the number of offenders who were convicted for a particular number of offenses, and the cumulative number and percent of offenses that were committed by the offenders. As illustrated, 205 of the Youngest cohort participants were convicted at least once (279 members had no convictions), and the number of offenses ranged from 1 to 33 offenses. Among the offenders, the modal category for offenses was one offense, although a smaller but comparable number of offenders had 2 (n=30) and 3 (n=28) offenses. In total, the Youngest cohort participants who were convicted accumulated a total of 1080 offenses between ages 10 and 30. Importantly, nearly

Table 2.5 Total number of offenses committed: Youngest cohort (TOTAL SAMPLE)

Number of offenses	Number of offenders	Cumulative % of men	Cumulative number of offenses	Cumulative % of offenses
0	279	57.6	0	0.0
1	40	65.9	40	3.7
2	30	72.1	100	9.3
3	28	77.9	184	17.0
4	19	81.8	260	24.0
5	17	85.3	345	31.9
6	15	88.4	435	40.3
7	11	90.7	512	47.4
8	9	92.6	584	54.1
9	5	93.6	629	58.2
10	3	94.2	659	61.0
11	7	95.7	736	68.1
12	4	96.5	784	72.6
13	3	97.1	823	76.2
14	2	97.5	851	78.8
15	1	97.7	866	80.2
16	4	98.6	930	86.1
18	3	99.2	984	91.1
19	1	99.4	1003	92.9
20	1	99.6	1023	94.7
24	1	99.8	1047	96.9
33	1	100.0	1080	100.0

Note: An important point to make here is that 5.8 % of the PYS Youngest cohort committed at least 10 offenses and they were responsible for 39.0 % of all of the offenses committed by the sample.

half (45 %) of the offenses were committed by 7.4 % of the participants. Figure 2.5 also displays a graphical depiction of the number of offenders by the number of offenses committed for the Youngest cohort.

Table 2.6 presents these same criminal career dimensions of participation and frequency but for the Oldest cohort. Specifically, 244 of the Oldest cohort participants were convicted at least once between ages 10 and 30, and an almost equal number ($n=243$) were not convicted during this time period. Again, the modal category for offenses was one offense ($n=61$), although the number of offenses ranged from 1 to 42 convictions. Importantly, 8.8 % of the participants committed nearly half of all of the offenses (49.7 %). Overall, the Oldest cohort offenders managed to accumulate 1437 offenses between ages 10 and 30. Figure 2.6 presents a line graph demonstrating the relationship between the number of offenders and the number of offenses committed for the Oldest cohort.

Additional criminal career dimensions including the percent recidivist, average number of offenses, average age at first offense, average age at last offense, and average criminal career length in duration in years is shown in Table 2.7 for the Youngest cohort active offenders. For example, approximately one-third (33.2 %) of the Youngest cohort active offenders had their first offense at ages 10–14, and

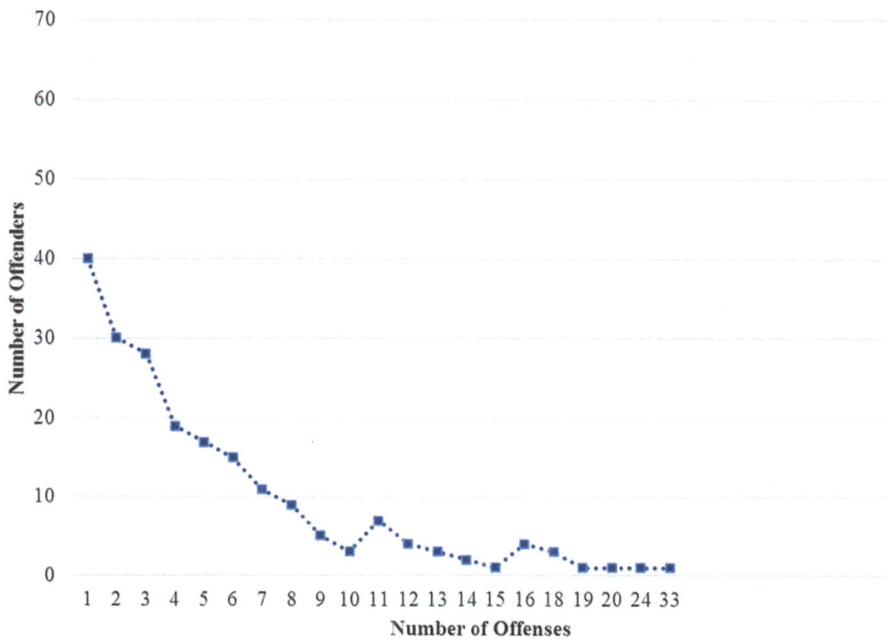

Fig. 2.5 Number of offenders related to number of offenses: Youngest cohort (ACTIVE OFFENDERS)

among these active offenders, 63.2 % recidivated at ages 15–18, 67.7 % recidivated at ages 19–24, and 42.7 % recidivated at ages 25–30. Furthermore, these active offenders with an onset age between 10 and 14 accumulated an average of 8.07 offenses between ages 10 and30, with an average age at first offense of 13.04, an average age at last offense of 23.03, and an average career length of 9.99 years.

Comparatively, these additional criminal career dimensions are displayed in Table 2.8 for the Oldest cohort active offenders. For instance, the age of onset for 27.9 % of the Oldest cohort active offenders was between 10 and 14 years old, and among those whose onset age was during this age band, 72.1 % recidivated during ages 15–18, 67.7 % recidivated during ages 19–24, and 44.1 % recidivated during ages 25–30. Furthermore, this group averaged slightly more than 10 offenses ($M = 10.15$) between the ages 10–30, with an average age of onset of 13.34, and average age at last offense of 22.44, with an average criminal career length of 9.10 years.

Beyond the comparisons that were made by onset age group, it is also important to more fully explore the relationship between offense frequency and age at first offense, age at last offense, and average criminal career length. For this portion of the analysis, the active offenders are categorized based on their offense frequency into the following categories: one offense, two offenses, 3–4 offenses, 5–9 offenses, 10–14 offenses, and 15+ offenses. For the Youngest cohort (Table 2.9), 40 men only had one offense between ages 10 and 30, and their average age of onset and age at last offense were obviously the same ($M = 21.53$ years). For those active offenders who had two offenses, their average age at first offense was 18.93 and their average

Table 2.6 Total number of offenses committed: Oldest cohort (TOTAL SAMPLE)

Number of offenses	Number of offenders	Cumulative % of men	Cumulative number of offenses	Cumulative % of offenses
0	243	49.9	0	0.0
1	61	62.4	61	4.2
2	31	68.8	123	8.6
3	24	73.7	195	13.6
4	21	78.0	279	19.4
5	13	80.7	344	23.9
6	17	84.2	446	31.0
7	15	87.3	551	38.3
8	6	88.5	599	41.7
9	6	89.7	653	45.4
10	7	91.2	723	50.3
11	4	92.0	767	53.4
12	7	93.4	851	59.2
13	10	95.5	981	68.3
14	2	95.9	1009	70.2
15	3	96.5	1054	73.3
16	1	96.7	1070	74.5
17	3	97.3	1121	78.0
19	2	97.7	1159	80.7
21	3	98.4	1222	85.0
22	2	98.8	1266	88.1
23	2	99.2	1312	91.3
26	1	99.4	1338	93.1
27	1	99.6	1365	95.0
30	1	99.8	1395	97.1
42	1	100.0	1437	100.0

Note: An important point to make here is that 8.8 % of the PYS Oldest cohort committed at least 10 offenses and they were responsible for 49.7 % of all of the offenses committed by the sample

age at last offense was 22.93 (average criminal career length=4 years). The Youngest cohort participants who committed 3–4 offenses, on average, began their criminal career at age 16.79 and had an average criminal career length of 6.23 years (average age at last offense=23.02). Comparatively, 61 of the Oldest cohort participants committed one offense during ages 10–30, and their average age at the time of this offense was 19.62 (Table 2.9). Among the two-time active offenders, their average age at first offense was 18.65, and their average age at last offense was 21.32 (average criminal career length=2.68 years). The Oldest cohort active offenders who committed 3–4 offenses had an average criminal career length of slightly more than 5 years (M=5.31 years), with an average age of 16.64 and 21.96 for their first and last offense.

In general, among the 205 active offenders in the Youngest cohort, their average age at first offense and age at last offense was 17.37 and 22.99, respectively, yielding an average criminal career length of 5.62 years, and the average age of onset for

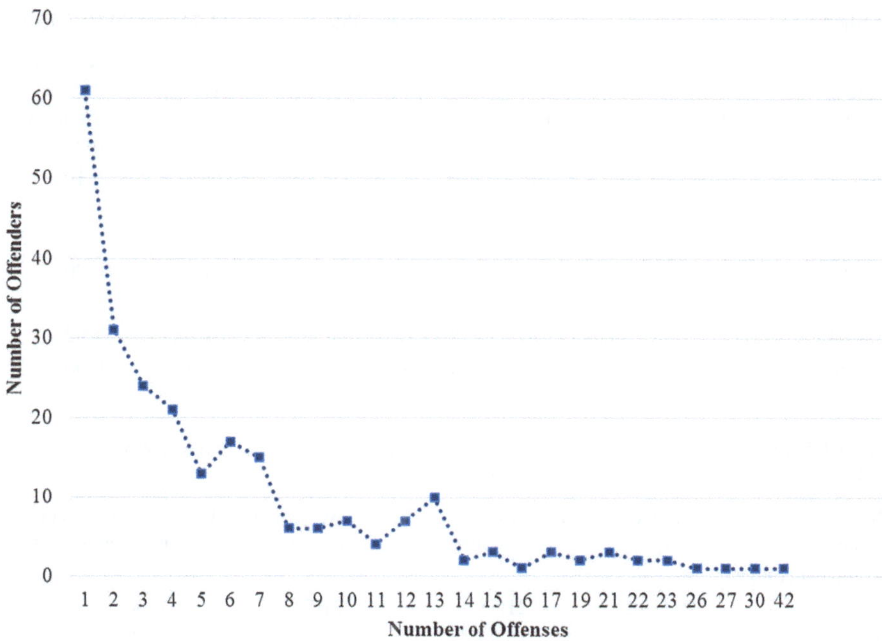

Fig. 2.6 Number of offenders related to number of offenses: Oldest cohort (ACTIVE OFFENDERS)

Table 2.7 Age of onset versus criminal career measures: Youngest cohort (ACTIVE OFFENDERS)

Age group at first offense	% of offenders	(%) Recidivist by age group	Average number of offenses (range)	Average age at first offense	Average age at last offense	Average career duration in years
10–14	33.2	15–18: (63.2)	8.07 (2–24)	13.04	23.03	9.99
		19–24: (67.7)				
		25–30: (42.7)				
15–18	35.1	19–24: (51.4)	5.00 (1–33)	16.38	21.22	4.85
		25–30: (26.4)				
19–24	21.5	25–30: (27.3)	2.89 (1–11)	21.05	23.50	2.45
25–30	10.2	n/a	2.10 (1–5)	27.10	27.90	0.81

the 244 Oldest cohort active offenders was 17.02 and their average age at last offense was 21.90 (average criminal career length: 4.87 years). Turning toward the following categories, which all meet the typical 5 or more offenses threshold for chronic offending (cf. Wolfgang et al. 1972), the average onset ages were 15.91 (Youngest and Oldest cohorts) for the active offenders who committed 5–9 offenses, 14.42 (Youngest cohort) and 14.93 (Oldest cohort) for the active offenders who committed 10–14 offenses, and 13.50 (Youngest cohort) and 13.75 (Oldest cohort) for the active offenders who committed 15+ offenses, respectively.

Table 2.8 Age of onset versus criminal career measures: Oldest cohort (ACTIVE OFFENDERS)

Age group at first offense	% of offenders	(%) Recidivist by age group	Average number of offenses (range)	Average age at first offense	Average age at last offense	Average career duration in years
10–14	27.9	15–18: (72.1)	10.15 (1–42)	13.34	22.44	9.10
		19–24: (67.7)				
		25–30: (44.1)				
15–18	45.5	19–24: (46.9)	5.14 (1–30)	16.22	20.41	4.20
		25–30: (19.8)				
19–24	22.1	25–30: (27.8)	3.00 (1–13)	21.28	23.20	1.92
25–30	4.5	n/a	1.36 (1–4)	27.09	27.09	0.00

Table 2.9 Frequency of offending versus criminal careers: Youngest and Oldest cohorts (ACTIVE OFFENDERS)

Number of offenses	Number of men (%)	Average age at first offense	Average age at last offense	Average career duration in years
Youngest cohort				
1	40 (19.5)	21.53	21.53	0.00
2	30 (14.6)	18.93	22.93	4.00
3–4	47 (22.9)	16.79	23.02	6.23
5–9	57 (27.8)	15.91	23.33	7.42
10–14	19 (9.3)	14.42	23.79	9.37
15+	12 (5.9)	13.50	25.08	11.58
Total	205	17.37	22.99	5.62
Oldest cohort				
1	61 (25.0)	19.62	19.62	0.00
2	31 (12.7)	18.65	21.32	2.68
3–4	45 (18.4)	16.64	21.96	5.31
5–9	57 (23.4)	15.91	22.60	6.68
10–14	30 (12.3)	14.93	23.53	8.60
15+	20 (8.2)	13.75	25.15	11.40
Total	244	17.02	21.90	4.87

2.6 Categories of Official Offenders

Tables 2.10 and 2.11 provide a detailed breakdown for a variety of offender categories that were constructed in order to further dissect the official offending patterns of the Youngest cohort and the Oldest cohort PYS participants, respectively. Among the Youngest cohort, 279 were not convicted between ages 10 and 30, whereas 205 of the participants were convicted at least once during this time period. Nearly two-thirds of the Youngest cohort (66.3 %) had not accumulated a conviction by the age of 20, and 28.7 % were convicted between ages 21 and 30. Among the offenders, specifically, 32.2 % were only convicted up to age 20, 21.9 % were only convicted

Table 2.10 Categories of official offenders: Youngest cohort (TOTAL SAMPLE and ACTIVE OFFENDERS)

Category	Number of men	% of total sample (% of offenders only)
Not convicted	279	57.6
Convicted	205	42.4
Not convicted up to 20	331	66.3
Convicted up to 20	168	33.7
Not convicted at 21+	345	71.3
Convicted at 21+	139	28.7
Convicted only up to 20	66	(32.2)
Convicted only at 21+	45	(21.9)
Convicted before and after 21	94	(45.9)
One-time offender	40	(19.5)
Recidivist	165	(80.5)
Non-chronic offender (<5 offenses)	117	(57.1)
Chronic offender (5+ offenses)	88	(42.9)
Career duration <15 years	189	(93.5)
Career duration 15 years+	16	(7.8)

Table 2.11 Categories of official offenders: Oldest cohort (TOTAL SAMPLE and ACTIVE OFFENDERS)

Category	Number of men	% of total sample (% of offenders only)
Not convicted	243	49.9
Convicted	244	50.1
Not convicted up to 20	291	57.9
Convicted up to 20	212	42.1
Not convicted at 21+	353	72.5
Convicted at 21+	134	27.5
Convicted only up to 20	110	(45.1)
Convicted only at 21+	43	(17.6)
Convicted before and after 21	91	(37.3)
One-time offender	61	(25.0)
Recidivist	183	(75.0)
Non-chronic offender (<5 offenses)	137	(56.1)
Chronic offender (5+ offenses)	107	(43.9)
Career duration <15 years	231	(94.7)
Career duration 15 years+	13	(5.3)

at ages 21–30, and 45.9 % were convicted both before age 21 and after age 21. Approximately, four out of every five of the offenders recidivated at some point, and the majority of these offenders (57.1 %) were not classified as chronic offenders as they had accumulated less than five offenses at ages 10–30. In addition, only 7.8 % of the Youngest cohort offenders had a criminal career length of 15 years of greater.

Roughly equivalent percentages of Oldest cohort participants were offenders (50.1 %) and non-offenders (49.9 %). A noticeable majority (57.9 %) of the Oldest cohort participants were not convicted up to age 20, and slightly more than one out of every four of the Oldest cohort participants were convicted between ages 21 and 30. Among the offenders, specifically, 45.1 % were only convicted between ages 10 and 20, 17.6 % were only convicted between ages 21and 30, and 37.3 % were convicted both between ages 10 and 20 and ages 21–30. Exactly three out of every four of the offenders recidivated at some point, although greater than half of the offenders (56.1 %) did not meet the five or more offenses threshold to be categorized as chronic offenders. Finally, only 5.3 % of the Oldest cohort offenders had a criminal career length of 15 years or greater.

2.7 Summary

This chapter presented a rich amount of official offending information for the PYS Youngest and Oldest cohorts, and some of the main highlights are summarized here. The overall prevalence of offending for the Youngest cohort was 42.4 %, with estimates ranging from 14.5 % (ages 10–14) to 26.5 % (ages 19–24) for various age bands and from 13.0 % (serious theft) to 20.7 % (serious violence) for the various types of crime, whereas the overall prevalence of offending for the Oldest cohort was 50.1 %, with estimates ranging from 14.6 % (ages 10–14) to 34.0 % (ages 15–18) for the age bands and from 19.9 % (moderate violence) to 32.9 % (moderate theft) for the crime types. The Youngest cohort accumulated 1080 offenses, and the Oldest cohort accumulated 1437 offenses between ages 10 and 30, and considerable continuity in offending was observed. Age at first offense, age at last offense, and criminal career length was found to vary based on age-band of onset (e.g., ages 10–14, ages 15–18, ages 19–24, or ages 25–30) from 13.04 to 27.10, 21.22 to 27.90, and 0.81 to 9.99 years for the Youngest cohort active offenders and from 13.34 to 27.09, 20.41 to 27.09, and 0.00 to 9.10 years for the Oldest cohort active offenders. Active offenders with the greatest number of offenses (15+) had the lengthiest criminal careers, averaging 11.58 years for the Youngest cohort and 11.40 for the Oldest cohort. Finally, for the Youngest cohort, 33.7 % were convicted up to age 20, 28.7 % were convicted at ages 21–30, and among the Youngest cohort active offenders, 45.9 % were convicted both before and after age 21, 80.5 % were recidivists, 42.9 % were chronic offenders (e.g., committed 5+ offenses), and 7.8 % had a criminal career length of 15+ years. Among the Oldest cohort, 42.1 % were convicted up to age 20, 27.5 % were convicted at ages 21–30, and among the Oldest cohort active offenders, 37.3 % were convicted both before and after age 21, 75.0 % were recidivists, 43.9 % were chronic offenders (e.g., committed 5+ offenses), and 5.3 % had a criminal career length of 15+ years.

Chapter 3
Self-Reported Criminal Careers

3.1 Measurement of Self-Reported Offending in the PYS

Self-reported offending in the PYS was primarily assessed using the 40-item Self-Reported Delinquency (SRD) scale, which was derived from the frequently used and previously validated Elliot et al. (1985) scale from the National Youth Survey. Furthermore, this scale was modified for the Causes and Correlates of Delinquency Program (Loeber et al. 1998). For each of the 40 items in the SRD scale, the participants were asked to report whether they had committed the specific act in the previous year, and if so, how many times they had committed the act in the previous year. For analytic purposes, the SRD scale relied on here is based on five crime types that have been utilized frequently in the literature when using data from the PYS (see Loeber et al. 2008). Specifically, *moderate theft* is defined as stealing a bicycle or skateboard from the street, stealing things worth more than $5, joyriding, purse snatching, dealing in stolen goods, or stealing from a car; *serious theft* refers to breaking and entering or auto theft; *moderate violence* is gang fighting; *serious violence* is defined as forcible robbery, attacking with intent to injure, sexual coercion, or rape; and *drug dealing* is defined as the selling of marijuana or hard drugs (for more detailed information on the assessment methods for how and when the self-report data was collected and coded, see Loeber et al. 2008; Theobald et al. 2014).

Prior to moving into a detailed discussion of the self-report offending of the PYS Youngest and Oldest cohorts, it is necessary to provide some background information regarding the timing of the self-report offending assessments and how these assessments varied by age (and at times by cohort). For instance, initially, the participants were followed up half-yearly (seven assessments for the Youngest cohort and five assessments for the Oldest cohort), but because of reasons of finances and burden to the participants and staff, a yearly interview schedule was subsequently instituted. These half-yearly assessments were summed for the analyses to yearly assessments. Table 3.1 shows the yearly assessments on which the self-report offending analyses detailed below for each cohort are based.

© The Authors 2016

W.G. Jennings et al., *Offending from Childhood to Young Adulthood*,
SpringerBriefs in Criminology, DOI 10.1007/978-3-319-25966-6_3

Table 3.1 Sample sizes by self-report assessment/age for Youngest and Oldest cohorts

	Youngest cohort	Oldest cohort
Age 10		
Valid responses	431	0
Not assessed	46	506
Missing	26	0
Age 11		
Valid responses	467	21
Not assessed	1	485
Missing	35	0
Age 12		
Valid responses	472	245
Not assessed	0	261
Missing	31	0
Age 13		
Valid responses	462	426
Not assessed	0	77
Missing	41	3
Age 14		
Valid responses	457	480
Not assessed	0	5
Missing	46	21
Age 15		
Valid responses	445	462
Not assessed	0	0
Missing	58	44
Age 16		
Valid responses	434	447
Not assessed	0	0
Missing	69	59
Age 17		
Valid responses	430	436
Not assessed	0	0
Missing	73	70
Age 18		
Valid responses	423	450
Not assessed	0	0
Missing	80	56
Age 19		
Valid responses	318	445
Not assessed	116	0
Missing	69	61
Age 20		
Valid responses	67	436
Not assessed	424	0

(continued)

Table 3.1 (continued)

	Youngest cohort	Oldest cohort
Missing	12	70
Age 21		
Valid responses	0	443
Not assessed	503	0
Missing	0	63
Age 22		
Valid responses	0	444
Not assessed	503	0
Missing	0	62
Age 23		
Valid responses	38	440
Not assessed	386	0
Missing	79	66
Age 24		
Valid responses	137	428
Not assessed	286	1
Missing	80	77
Age 25		
Valid responses	148	259
Not assessed	276	190
Missing	79	57
Age 26		
Valid responses	89	93
Not assessed	353	390
Missing	61	23
Age 27		
Valid responses	116	13
Not assessed	325	492
Missing	62	1
Age 28		
Valid responses	136	0
Not assessed	305	506
Missing	62	0
Age 29		
Valid responses	100	0
Not assessed	301	506
Missing	102	0
Age 30		
Valid responses	38	0
Not assessed	364	506
Missing	101	0

Table 3.1 also provides the following information for each cohort for each age: the number of valid cases/participants, the number of cases/participants that were not assessed, and the number of cases/participants where data was missing. Recognizing that the overall sample size of the Youngest PYS cohort is 503, the range of valid cases from ages 10 to 30 ranged from 38 to 472, and there were two particular ages (ages 21 and 22) where *no* participants were assessed and no data were collected. Missing data in any given year ranged from 12 to 102 cases, which was relatively low considering the length of the follow-up (21 years). Furthermore, for the most part, the participants were assessed and the data was fairly complete for the Youngest cohort for ages 10–19, and then the number of cases/participants assessed noticeably declined. Comparatively, no participants in the Oldest cohort were assessed at age 10 or at ages 28–30, and the range of valid cases spanned from 13 to 480 (overall sample size of the Oldest PYS cohort is 506). Missing data in any given year was also fairly low ranging from 0 to 77 cases. In general, the Oldest cohort participants were regularly assessed, and the data was fairly complete from ages 13 to 25 before dropping off noticeably at ages 26 and 27 (again, no participants were assessed at ages 28–30).

Provided with this information, we would like to caution readers when reviewing and reading through the analyses in this chapter to bear in mind these assessment issues noted above (and how these issues differ by cohort) when interpreting the results. Furthermore, for descriptive and comparative purposes and to be consistent with Farrington et al. (2013), we utilize the same age bands (ages 10–14, ages 15–18, ages 19–24, and ages 25–30) that were relied on in the previous chapter on official records to present the corresponding estimates for self-reported offending in the analysis that follows in this chapter. However, rather than using only the cases/participants that were assessed and not missing data at each and every age for a given age band (which would likely lead to a serious selection bias concern and a greatly deflated sample size for analysis), we allowed all of the participants to contribute any and all of their self-reported offending information that was available to the estimates derived for a particular age band (e.g., being an active offender at any age(s) in a given age-band results in that participant being a contributor to the self-reported offending estimates for that particular age band).

Nevertheless, it is still important to acknowledge that this practice described above may have led to somewhat conservative estimates of self-reported offending for any given age-band estimate, and the estimates that are more prone to this concern are the ages 19–24 and ages 25–30 estimates for the Youngest cohort. Specifically, none of the Youngest cohort participants were assessed, and no data was collected for ages 21 and 22, and the number of the Youngest cohort participants who were assessed and had valid data at age 20 and beyond ranged from 38 to 116. In contrast, the age-band estimates that are in need of qualifying for the Oldest cohort are the ages 10–14 and ages 25–30 estimates as no Oldest cohort participants were assessed at age 10 or at ages 28–30, and very few were assessed at ages 11 and 27. As such, a strict interpretation would be that the self-report offending data is based on ages 10–20 and 23–30 for the Youngest cohort and ages 11–27 for the Oldest cohort.

Table 3.2 Prevalence of self-reported offenders: Youngest and Oldest cohorts (TOTAL SAMPLE)

Offense type	Percent at age				All ages
	10–14	15–18	19–24	25–30	
Youngest cohort					
Moderate theft	31.1	30.6	6.5	7.6	44.9
Serious theft	11.8	10.7	1.0	0.8	15.7
Moderate violence	21.6	8.6	0.8	0.5	20.3
Serious violence	15.1	11.2	2.1	1.3	18.0
Drug dealing	14.2	27.5	16.4	14.9	37.8
Any theft, violence, or drug dealing	41.1	36.1	19.4	19.4	56.3
Oldest cohort					
Moderate theft	35.3	51.5	33.8	2.5	67.8
Serious theft	14.9	18.3	8.3	0.0	28.9
Moderate violence	20.9	23.1	13.7	0.2	35.2
Serious violence	14.5	21.0	17.7	1.4	34.0
Drug dealing	6.4	31.2	39.8	4.5	47.4
Any theft, violence, or drug dealing	47.4	64.0	56.0	6.8	76.5

3.2 Prevalence of Self-Reported Offending

Table 3.2 displays the prevalence of self-reported offending in the PYS for the Youngest and Oldest cohorts by age bands (i.e., ages 10–14, ages 15–18, ages 19–24, and ages 25–30) and by crime type (e.g., moderate theft, serious theft, moderate violence, serious violence, and drug dealing) as well as overall prevalence estimates. Overall, from ages 10–30, moderate theft was the most prevalent form of self-reported offending for the Youngest (44.9 %) and Oldest cohorts (67.8 %), followed by drug dealing (Youngest cohort, 37.8 %; Oldest cohort, 47.4 %). In addition, prevalence estimates of self-reported offending in general declined over age from 41.1 % at ages 10–14, 36.1 % at ages 15–18, and 19.4 % at ages 19–24 and ages 25–30 with an overall prevalence estimate of 56.3 % for any involvement in any type of crime during any particular age band from ages 10 to 30 for the Youngest cohort. Comparatively, an overall prevalence estimate of 76.5 % was obtained for the Oldest cohort for any involvement in any type of crime during any particular age band from ages 10 to 30, with the following age-band-specific prevalence estimates: 47.4 % (ages 10–14), 64.0 % (ages 15–18), 56.0 % (ages 19–24), and 6.8 % (ages 25–30).

There are a series of noteworthy cohort differences regarding these prevalence estimates in need of highlighting here. For example, the Oldest cohort self-reported a substantively higher prevalence of involvement in offending at ages 15–18 and ages 19–24 as well as overall (ages 10–30). In contrast, the Youngest cohort had a higher prevalence of self-reported involvement in offending at ages 25–30; however, bear in mind that the Oldest cohort was not assessed at ages 28–30. Thus, their prevalence estimate for this age band is a conservative estimate confined to ages

25–27. Ages 10–14 self-reported involvement in offending was fairly comparable between the two cohorts. In addition, this trend of the Oldest cohort self-reporting greater involvement in offending was generally observed across the various types of crime, particularly for all of the crime types at ages 19–24.

3.3 Continuity in Self-Reported Offending

Beyond the general prevalence estimates of self-reported offending by age bands and crime type for the two PYS cohorts, there was also evidence of a significant degree of continuity in self-reported offending across the age bands. Specifically, Table 3.3 displays these continuity estimates by age bands and reports Odds Ratios for age-band comparisons for the Youngest and Oldest cohorts for moderate and serious levels of offending. Approximately, 58.8 % and 78.6 % of the Youngest and Oldest cohorts, respectively, who self-reported offending at ages 10–14 also self-reported offending at ages of 15–18, 16.5 % (Youngest cohort) and 57.1 % (Oldest cohort) who self-reported offending at ages 15–18 also self-reported offending at ages 19–24, and 25.0 % (Youngest cohort) and 6.1 % (Oldest cohort) who self-reported offending at ages 19–24 also self-reported offending at ages 25–30. Overall, the corresponding Odds Ratios revealed statistically significant evidence for continuity in self-reported offending across the various age-band comparisons for both PYS cohorts with the Odds Ratios ranging from 2.5 to 9.7 (Youngest cohort) and 1.1–6.4 (Oldest cohort).

Table 3.3 Continuity in self-reported offending: Youngest and Oldest cohorts (ACTIVE OFFENDERS)

Age 1	Age 2	Age 1 and Age 2	Age 2 and not Age 1	OR
Youngest cohort				
10–14	15–18	58.8 % (*n*=77)	20.3 % (*n*=44)	5.6
10–14	19–24	15.8 % (*n*=22)	1.9 % (*n*=4)	9.7
10–14	25–30	12.6 % (*n*=17)	6.6 % (*n*=14)	2.5
15–18	19–24	16.5 % (*n*=20)	2.3 % (*n*=5)	8.3
15–18	25–30	13.8 % (*n*=15)	3.9 % (*n*=8)	3.9
19–24	25–30	25.0 % (*n*=7)	7.1 % (*n*=23)	4.3
Oldest cohort				
10–14	15–18	78.6 % (*n*=125)	43.1 % (*n*=88)	4.9
10–14	19–24	57.0 % (*n*=90)	30.6 % (*n*=57)	3.0
10–14	25–30	5.7 % (*n*=11)	1.7 % (*n*=4)	3.4
15–18	19–24	57.1 % (*n*=108)	17.2 % (*n*=21)	6.4
15–18	25–30	5.0 % (*n*=10)	0.0 % (*n*=0)	1.1
19–24	25–30	6.1 % (*n*=9)	1.0 % (*n*=2)	6.2

Note: Age 1 and Age 2 = percentage of those who offended at age 1, who also offended at age 2; Age 2 and not Age 1 = percentage of those who did not offend at age 1, but who offended at age 2; OR = Odds Ratio (all ORs are statistically significant, $p<0.05$, one tailed).

3.4 Prior Research Comparing Official and Self-Reported Offending

There has been much discussion and debate in the criminological literature as to using official data and/or self-report data to measure offending (see Loeber et al. 2008; Thornberry and Krohn 2000). For example, some have argued that official data only represents the "tip of the iceberg" as much of the crime that is committed does not come to the attention of law enforcement. Comparatively, self-reported offending sources have been described as being better able to capture a more accurate portrait of the true number of offenses committed. However, self-report data have also been criticized as some doubt the validity and truthfulness of self-reports as some people may choose to conceal or not report offending, exaggerate or underinflate their offending, or not report at all due to memory lapse or inaccurate recall. Despite these latter concerns, many scholars have carried out methodological assessments establishing internal consistency, retest stability, and concurrent predictive validity of self-reported offending (Farrington 1973), as well as tackling other methodological issues concerning self-reported offending (Hindelang et al. 1981; Huizinga and Elliott 1986; Farrington et al. 1996; Jolliffe and Farrington 2014; Junger-Tas and Marshall 1999; Krohn et al. 2010; Lauritsen 1998; Osgood et al. 2002; Piquero et al. 2002; Thornberry and Krohn 2000).

Farrington (1973) performed one of the few and earliest studies to examine the predictive validity of self-reported offending in relation to official offending. His analysis of data from the Cambridge Study in Delinquent Development (CSDD) revealed that, among boys that had no convictions, a measure of self-reported offending at age 14 was a significant predictor of official convictions in the next 3 years. For example, 20 % of the boys who were not convicted of burglary prior to age 18, but self-reported having committed burglary, were convicted of burglary by age 32, whereas only 2 % of those boys who were not convicted of burglary by age 18 and denied having committed burglary were convicted of burglary by age 32. In fact, Farrington reported that only 23 boys (6 % of the sample) self-reported not having committed any theft of and from vehicles, assault, vandalism, drug use, or shoplifting offenses prior to age 18, and none of these boys were convicted up to age 32. Farrington concluded that this provides strong evidence that these boys were likely telling the truth regarding their offending behavior.

More recently, Farrington et al. (2003) compared the official and self-reported offending of youth participants in the Seattle Social Development Project from ages 11 to17. A number of interesting findings emerged. First, the authors reported that the prevalence of official and self-reported offending increased with age (see, e.g., Loeber et al. 2015). Second, offending frequency increased with age, whereas official offending remained more constant. Third, there was a considerable amount of continuity observed for both official and self-reported offending. Fourth, an early age of onset was a significant predictor of offending frequency, and this relationship was observed for both official offending and self-reported offending. In addition Loeber et al. (2008) have also reported systematic comparisons of self-reports and official offending in the Pittsburgh Youth Study (PYS) for theft and violence offenses specifically (see also Theobald et al. 2014). Their results indicated that, in the Youngest cohort, 31 % and 32 % of those who self-reported serious violence and/or serious theft were also convicted for serious violence and/or serious theft, respectively. Among the Oldest cohort, 30 % of those who self-reported serious violence were also convicted for serious violence, and 52 % of those who self-reported serious theft were also convicted for serious theft.

Farrington et al. (2013) offered one of the most recent, and arguably the most comprehensive, comparisons to date of official and self-reported offending among CSDD participants from adolescence into late middle age and computed self-report-to-official-offending ratios to permit the scaling up from official delinquency records to self-reported delinquency. Their results demonstrated self-report-to-official-offending ratios that ranged from 5.8 (burglary) to 4159.8 (drug use) for specific types of crime. Overall, Farrington et al. reported that, across all ages and crime types, the CSDD males self-reported committing 38.7 offenses for every one officially recorded offense. Finally, once Farrington et al. restricted the sample to only consider those males who were convicted, the self-report-to-official-offending ratios ranged from 2.8 (burglary) to 20.7 (assault) and from 2.4 (ages 42–47) to 24.1 (ages 15–18).

3.5 Scaling Up Offending Estimates

Based on these important results, Table 3.4 provides the ratio of self-reported offenses to official offenses for the Youngest and Oldest cohort offenders. These self-report-to-official-offending ratios are also presented by crime type (e.g., moderate theft, serious theft, moderate violence, serious violence, drug dealing) and overall across all crime types and ages 10–30. Among the Youngest cohort offenders, the largest ratio is for drug dealing, where for every one drug dealing officially recorded offense, the Youngest cohort offenders self-reported having committed 330.98 drug dealing offenses. The ratio declined considerably for the other offenses with ratios of 25.89 for moderate theft, 10.50 for moderate violence, 6.21 for serious theft, and 5.72 for serious violence. These ratios are also illustrated in Fig. 3.1. Across all crime types and ages 10–30, the Youngest cohort accumulated an average of 3.11 officially recorded offenses compared to self-reporting having committed an average of 326.86 offenses, yielding an overall self-report-to-official-offending ratio of 105.10.

For the Oldest cohort, drug dealing again revealed the largest self-report-to-official-offending ratio of 862.45 self-reported drug dealing offenses for every one drug dealing officially recorded offense. The ratios for the other crime types in descending order of magnitude were as follows: 41.80 for moderate theft, 7.70 for serious theft, 13.86 for moderate violence, and 6.86 for serious violence. These ratios are also illustrated in Fig. 3.1. Overall, across all crime types and ages 10–30, for every 1 officially recorded offense, the Oldest cohort participants self-reported having committed 130.24 offenses (Table 3.4).

Table 3.4 Ratio of self-reported to official offenses: Youngest and Oldest cohorts (ACTIVE OFFENDERS)

Offense type	Self-reported average	Official average	Ratio
Youngest cohort			
Moderate theft	25.11	0.97	25.89
Serious theft	2.61	0.42	6.21
Moderate violence	5.46	0.52	10.50
Serious violence	3.43	0.60	5.72
Drug dealing	290.25	0.61	330.98
Any theft, violence, or drug dealing	326.86	3.11	105.10
Oldest cohort			
Moderate theft	44.73	1.07	41.80
Serious theft	6.08	0.79	7.70
Moderate violence	4.02	0.29	13.86
Serious violence	2.95	0.43	6.86
Drug dealing	327.73	0.38	862.45
Any theft, violence, or drug dealing	385.51	2.96	130.24

Note: Self-reported crime-type averages may not necessarily sum to the self-reported any theft, violence, or drug dealing (all ages) total due to missing data. The overall self-reported-to-official-offending ratio excluding drug dealing (e.g., based on any theft or violence at all ages) is 14.64 for the Youngest cohort and 22.40 for the Oldest cohort.

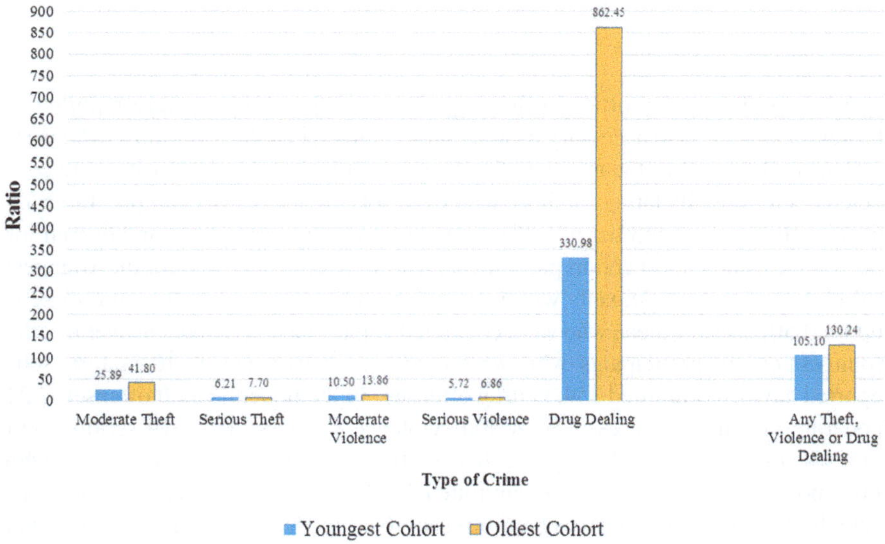

Fig. 3.1 Ratio of self-reported to official offenses: Youngest and Oldest cohorts (ACTIVE OFFENDERS)

Table 3.5 Number and ratio of self-reported offenses, by conviction status: Youngest and Oldest cohorts (CONVICTED OFFENDERS AND NON-CONVICTED OFFENDERS)

Offenses	Convicted self-reported average	Not convicted self-reported average	Ratio of self-reported offenses for convicted vs. not convicted
Youngest cohort			
Moderate theft	30.89	3.84	8.04
Serious theft	3.19	0.48	6.64
Moderate violence	7.24	0.47	15.40
Serious violence	4.84	0.16	30.25
Drug dealing	354.39	45.68	7.76
Any theft, violence, or drug dealing	400.56	51.63	7.76
Oldest cohort			
Moderate theft	57.05	16.51	3.45
Serious theft	7.87	2.19	3.59
Moderate violence	5.82	0.76	7.66
Serious violence	3.58	1.19	3.01
Drug dealing	526.83	36.29	14.52
Any theft, violence, or drug dealing	606.42	55.09	11.01

Note: Self-reported crime-type averages may not necessarily sum to the self-reported any theft, violence, or drug dealing (all ages) total due to missing data. The overall self-reported offenses ratio for those convicted and not convicted excluding drug dealing (e.g., based on any theft or violence at all ages) is 9.33 for the Youngest cohort and 4.23 for the Oldest cohort.

As the self-report-to-official-offending ratios discussed above were reported in the aggregate, it is also necessary to study these ratios specifically for those who were convicted of crimes, as the number of self-reported offenses for those who were convicted is substantially larger for those who were not convicted. For example, Table 3.5 displays the average number of self-reported offenses by crime type, and overall for the Youngest and Oldest cohort participants who were convicted and for the Youngest and Oldest cohort participants who were not convicted as well as the ratio of self-reported offenses for those who were convicted versus not convicted. On average, the Youngest cohort participants who were convicted between ages 10 and 30 self-reported having committed 354.39 drug offenses, 30.89 moderate theft offenses, 7.24 moderate violence offenses, 4.84 serious violence offenses, and 3.19 serious theft offenses compared to the Youngest cohort participants who were not convicted who self-reported, on average, having committed 45.68 drug dealing offenses, 3.84 moderate theft offenses, 0.48 serious theft offenses, 0.47 moderate violence offenses, and 0.16 for serious violence offenses (Fig. 3.2). Collectively, the convicted offenders self-reported an average of 400.56 offenses at ages 10–30 compared with 51.63 self-reported offenses for those who were not convicted. Ratios for all of these self-report comparisons can be found in Table 3.5 as well.

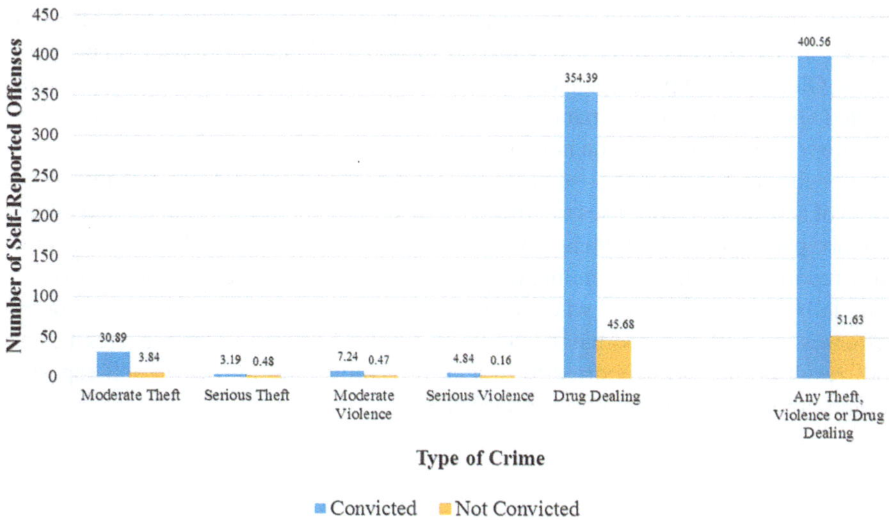

Fig. 3.2 Number of self-reported offenses, by conviction status: Youngest cohort (CONVICTED OFFENDERS AND NON-CONVICTED OFFENDERS)

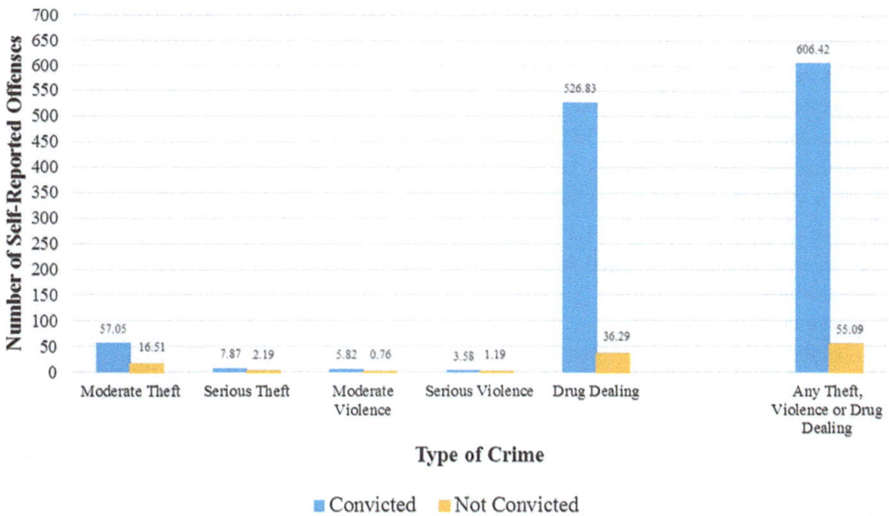

Fig. 3.3 Number of self-reported offenses, by conviction status: Oldest cohort (CONVICTED OFFENDERS AND NON-CONVICTED OFFENDERS)

A considerably large disparity was also observed in the number of self-reported offenses for the convicted offenders versus the not convicted offenders in the Oldest cohort (Table 3.5; Fig. 3.3). Specifically, the convicted offenders self-reported 526.83 drug dealing offenses, 57.05 moderate theft offenses, 7.87 serious theft offenses, 5.82 moderate violence offenses, and 3.58 serious violence offenses compared to the

36.29 drug dealing offenses, 16.51 moderate theft offenses, 2.19 serious theft offenses, 1.19 serious violence offenses, and 0.76 moderate violence offenses reported by those Oldest cohort participants that were not convicted. Taken as a whole, the convicted Oldest cohort participants self-reported 606.42 offenses relative to the 55.09 self-reported offenses for the not convicted Oldest cohort participants.

For the final stage of the scaling up analysis, Table 3.6 and Fig. 3.4 reveal the ratio of self-reported offenses to official offenses only for those Youngest and Oldest cohort participants who were convicted. For the Youngest cohort, the overall self-reported-to-official offending ratio was 76.01 self-reported offenses for every 1 officially recorded offense, whereas the Oldest cohort had 5.89 officially recorded offenses and self-reported having committed 606.42 offenses between ages 10 and 30, resulting in a self-reported-to-official-offending ratio of 102.93 self-reported offenses for every 1 officially recorded offense.

Table 3.6 Ratio of self-reported to official offenses among those who were convicted: Youngest and Oldest cohorts (CONVICTED OFFENDERS ONLY)

Offenses	Convicted self-reported average	Convicted official average	Convicted ratio of self-reported offenses to convictions
Youngest cohort			
Moderate theft	30.89	1.62	19.06
Serious theft	3.19	0.68	4.69
Moderate violence	7.24	0.86	8.41
Serious violence	4.84	1.16	4.17
Drug dealing	354.39	0.94	377.01
Any theft, violence, or drug dealing	400.56	5.27	76.01
Oldest cohort			
Moderate theft	57.05	1.96	29.11
Serious theft	7.87	1.32	5.96
Moderate violence	5.82	0.70	8.31
Serious violence	3.58	0.91	3.93
Drug dealing	526.83	1.00	526.83
Any theft, violence, or drug dealing	606.42	5.89	102.93

Note: Self-reported crime-type averages may not necessarily sum to the self-reported any theft, violence, or drug dealing (all ages) total due to missing data. The overall self-reported-to-official-offending ratio excluding drug dealing (e.g., based on any theft or violence at all ages) is 10.69 for the Youngest cohort and 16.28 for the Oldest cohort.

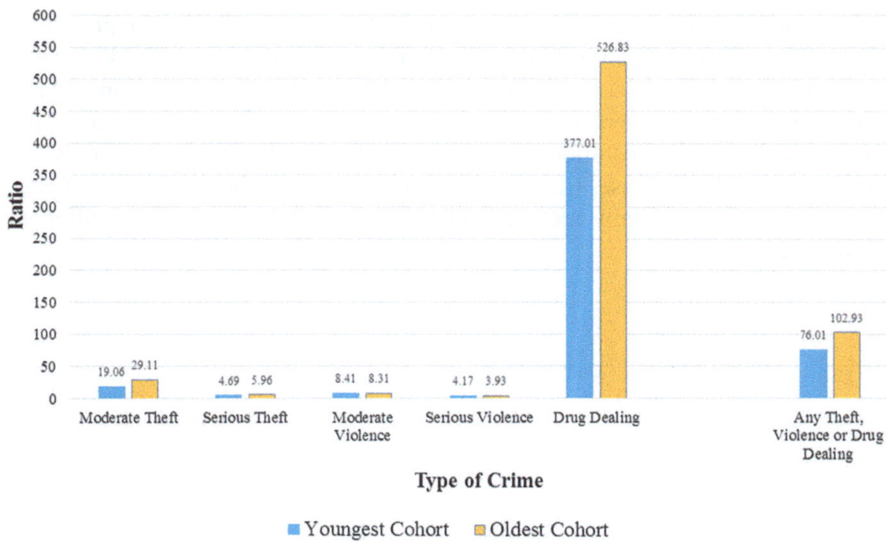

Fig. 3.4 Ratio of self-reported to official offenses among those who were convicted: Youngest and Oldest cohorts (CONVICTED OFFENDERS ONLY)

3.6 Summary

This chapter reported on a number of estimates derived from self-reports from the PYS Youngest and Oldest cohorts. The results suggested that the overall prevalence of self-reported offending for the Youngest cohort was 56.3 %, with estimates ranging by age from 19.4 % (ages 19–24 and ages 25–30) to 41.1 % (ages 10–14) for the various age bands and from 15.7 % (serious theft) to 44.9 % (moderate theft) for the various types of crime. For the Oldest cohort, the overall prevalence of self-reported offending was 76.5 %, the lowest prevalence was observed for ages 25–30 (6.8 %), and the highest prevalence was observed for ages 15–18 (64.0 %). Prevalence estimates also ranged from 28.9 % (serious theft) to 67.8 % (moderate theft) for the various crime types. Similar to what was demonstrated with the analysis using official data in the previous Chapter, the results show considerable evidence of continuity in offending for both the Youngest and the Oldest cohorts based on their self-reported offending.

Additional results from a series of scaling up exercises and calculations of self-reported-to-official-offending ratios yielded substantively meaningful comparisons between self-reported and official offending estimates. For instance, for the Youngest cohort, the overall ratio of self-reported-to-official offending was 105.10, or in other words for every 1 officially recorded conviction, the Youngest cohort participants self-reported having committed approximately 105 crimes. This self-reported-to-official-offending ratio was comparable for the Oldest cohort (ratio = 130.24). Finally, these ratios were also calculated after filtering out those PYS Youngest and Oldest cohort participants who were not convicted. These filtered analyses suggested that the Youngest cohort-convicted offenders averaged 5.27 officially recorded offenses and self-reported 400.56 offenses (ratio = 76.01) and the Oldest cohort-convicted offenders averaged 5.89 officially recorded offenses and self-reported 606.42 offenses (ratio = 102.96).

Chapter 4
Trajectories of Offending at Age 30

4.1 Group-Based Trajectory Modeling

What is much less known in the developmental/life-course criminological literature is the age(s) at which trajectories tend to crystallize or in other words how much of the life-course needs to be captured in a longitudinal analysis before the number of trajectories and the shape of the trajectories begin to stabilize (see Eggleston et al. 2004). In this vein, Jennings and Reingle (2012; see also Piquero 2008) have reported that across more than 100 trajectory-based studies, the number of groups ranges from two to seven, with most identifying three or four groups and most identifying trajectory groups consistent with Moffitt's (1993) adolescence-limited and life-course-persistent taxonomy. Yet, Farrington et al. (2013) are the only such study to date that has estimated trajectory models with a prospective longitudinal cohort of men at various age bands. Their results revealed two trajectory groups at ages 10–16 (non-offenders and adolescent-onset offenders), four trajectory groups at ages 10–24 (non-offenders, low adolescence peak, very low-rate chronic, and high adolescence peak), and five trajectory groups at ages 10–32, 10–40, 10–48, and 10–56 (non-offenders, low adolescence peak, very low-rate chronic, high adolescence peak, and high-rate chronic). And, as this implies, Farrington et al. (2013) reported there is a crystallization of trajectory groups (in number and shape) once offending data from ages 10 to 32 and beyond were incorporated.

Following Farrington et al.'s (2013) group-based trajectory model approach applied to official data from the Cambridge Study in Delinquency Development (CSDD), the trajectory analysis with the PYS conviction data proceeds in a series of stages. First, the trajectory models are estimated using the PROC TRAJ macro (Jones et al. 2001) whereby the trajectories are estimated in an iterative process across the modeling space for all potential parametric forms (constant, linear, quadratic, and cubic) and for all the possible number of trajectories until this process yields the most optimal trajectory solutions based on the maximization of the Bayesian information

© The Authors 2016

W.G. Jennings et al., *Offending from Childhood to Young Adulthood*,
SpringerBriefs in Criminology, DOI 10.1007/978-3-319-25966-6_4

criteria (BIC) and an examination of model precision through a review of the mean posterior probabilities of group assignment (Nagin 2005, 2010).

In recognition of the apparent skewness in the official data, the various iterations of the trajectory models are estimated utilizing the zero-inflated Poisson functional trajectory form, or commonly referred to as the ZIP model. Similarly, based on Farrington et al.'s (2013) strategy, the trajectories are estimated separately across three age bands {e.g., (1) ages 10–16, (2) ages 10–24, and (3) ages 10–30}, and, due to the PYS research design, these age-band trajectories are estimated separately for the Youngest and the Oldest cohorts (resulting in six trajectory models overall). Second, following the arrival at the most optimal trajectory solutions for the three age bands and for the two cohorts, a summary description is provided for the trajectory solutions with regard to the number of trajectory groups, their shape, and the prevalence of the Youngest and Oldest cohort participants in each trajectory group, respectively. In the final stage, a breakdown is reported for how the Youngest and Oldest cohort participants that are assigned to a particular group-based trajectory for any given age band (e.g., ages 10–16, ages 10–24, ages 10–30) are assigned across the subsequent identified age-band-trajectory groups, and a series of chi-square (χ^2) tests are employed to evaluate the significance of the association between one particular age-band-trajectory assignment with subsequent age-band-trajectory assignments.

4.2 Trajectory Model Fit

The quadratic parametric form was determined to be the most optimal form for all of the trajectory solutions, and the mean posterior probabilities of group assignment for the trajectories by PYS cohort, trajectory type, and across the three age bands are presented in Table 4.1. Nagin (2005) suggests a >0.70 threshold for the mean group-based posterior probabilities, and all of the trajectory solutions identified revealed mean group-based probabilities generally well above this threshold. For example, the mean group-based posterior probabilities for the Youngest cohort ranged from 0.91 to 0.97 (ages 10–16), 0.94–0.96 (ages 10–24), and 0.78–0.95 (ages 10–30), and these values ranged from 0.93 to 0.96 (ages 10–16), 0.85–0.95 (ages 10–24), and 0.81–0.95 for the Oldest cohort. All of these results suggest that the six trajectory solutions performed well as they were able to assign PYS participants to a group-based trajectory that best approximated their individual trajectory of offending with a high degree of accuracy.

4.3 Offending Trajectories: Ages 10–16

The prevalence/percent of PYS participants assigned to each trajectory group is displayed in Table 4.2 by trajectory type, across the three age bands, and by cohort. Figure 4.1 graphically illustrates the trajectories identified for the Youngest cohort based on their official offending data from ages 10 to 16. As can be seen, when only

Table 4.1 Mean group-based posterior probabilities by cohort, trajectory type, and across age bands from ages 10 to 30

	Youngest cohort	Youngest cohort	Youngest cohort	Oldest cohort	Oldest cohort	Oldest cohort
	Ages 10–16	Ages 10–24	Ages 10–30	Ages 10–16	Ages 10–24	Ages 10–30
Non-offenders	0.91 (0.90–0.92)	0.96 (0.95–0.97)	0.93 (0.92–0.94)	0.93 (0.93–0.94)	0.95 (0.94–0.96)	0.95 (0.94–0.96)
Adolescent onset	0.97 (0.96–0.99)	–	–	0.96 (0.93–0.97)	–	–
Very low-rate chronic	–	–	0.78 (0.75–0.82)	–	–	0.85 (0.83–0.88)
Low-rate adolescence peak	–	0.96 (0.95–0.97)	0.92 (0.90–0.94)	–	0.88 (0.86–0.90)	0.81 (0.77–0.84)
High-rate adolescence peak	–	0.94 (0.89–0.99)	0.95 (0.90–0.99)	–	0.91 (0.82–0.99)	0.92 (0.84–0.99)
High-rate chronic	–	–	–	–	0.85 (0.82–0.89)	0.90 (0.86–0.93)

Note: mean group-based posterior probabilities presented. Corresponding 95 % confidence intervals for mean group-based posterior probabilities in parentheses.

Table 4.2 Prevalence of trajectories by cohort, trajectory type, and across age bands from ages 10 to 30

	Youngest cohort	Youngest cohort	Youngest cohort	Oldest cohort	Oldest cohort	Oldest cohort
	Ages 10–16	Ages 10–24	Ages 10–30	Ages 10–16	Ages 10–24	Ages 10–30
Non-offenders	84.5 %	60.4 %	50.7 %	79.6 %	48.2 %	47.0 %
Adolescent onset	15.5 %	–	–	20.4 %	–	–
Very low-rate chronic	–	–	13.3 %	–	–	21.7 %
Low-rate adolescence peak	–	35.2 %	31.8 %	–	31.8 %	17.4 %
High-rate adolescence peak	–	4.4 %	4.2 %	–	3.2 %	3.0 %
High-rate chronic	–	–	–	–	16.8 %	10.9 %
Total	100.0 %	100.0 %	100.0 %	100.0 %	100.0 %	100.0 %

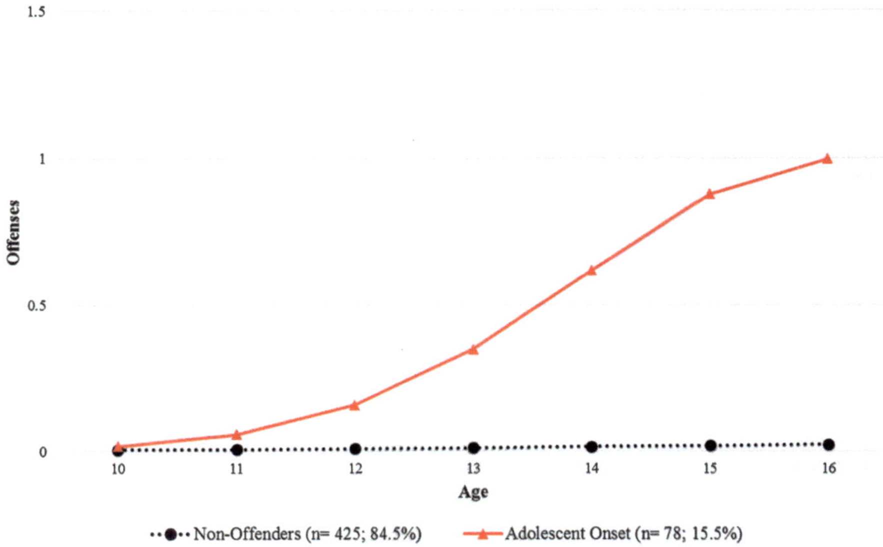

Fig. 4.1 PYS offending trajectories, ages 10–16: Youngest cohort

adolescent offending is considered, two trajectory groups best represent the Youngest cohort's offending patterns, essentially a non-offender group (84.5 %) and an adolescent-onset offender group (15.5 %). The adolescent-onset offender group begins offending at approximately age 11 and steadily increases throughout this adolescence time period from averaging nearly half of an offense per year to averaging one offense per year by age 16.

Comparatively, a similar two-group trajectory solution was identified for the Oldest cohort, with again a non-offender group who was the most prevalent (79.6 %) and an adolescent-onset offender group (Fig. 4.2). The adolescent-onset offender group comprised 20.4 % of the Oldest cohort and began offending at age 11 and increased precipitously over adolescence before peaking and averaging nearly 1.5 offenses a year at age 16, with much more variability toward mid- to late adolescence.

4.4 Offending Trajectories: Ages 10–24

Figure 4.3 provides the trajectory plots for the Youngest cohort based on official offending data from ages 10 to 24. Three trajectory groups were determined to provide the most optimal trajectory solution, where one group was considered a non-offender group (60.4 %), a second group was classified as a low-rate adolescence peak group (35.2 %), and the third group was a high-rate adolescence peak group (4.4 %). The low- and high-rate adolescence peak trajectories resembled one another in terms of their trends with an onset in early adolescence (ages 10–11), an increase throughout adolescence before peaking at ages 18–19, and then a decline

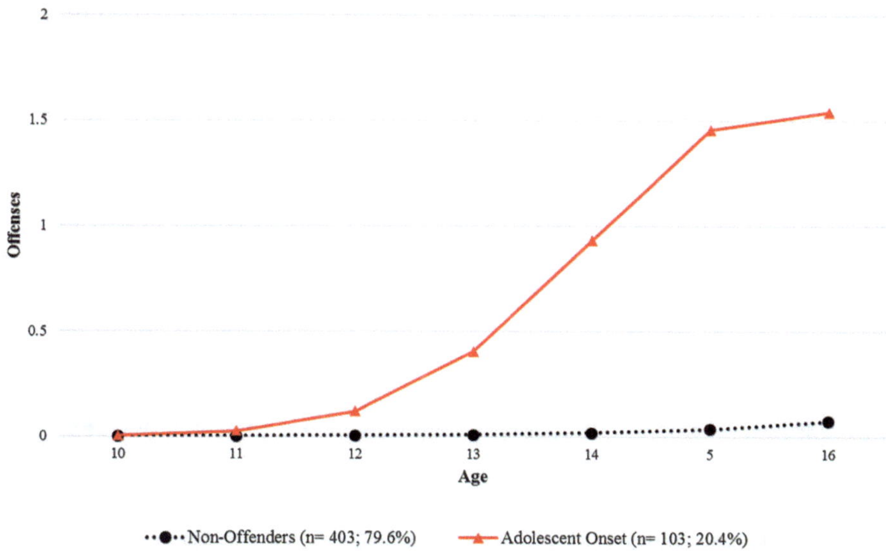

Fig. 4.2 PYS offending trajectories, ages 10–16: Oldest cohort

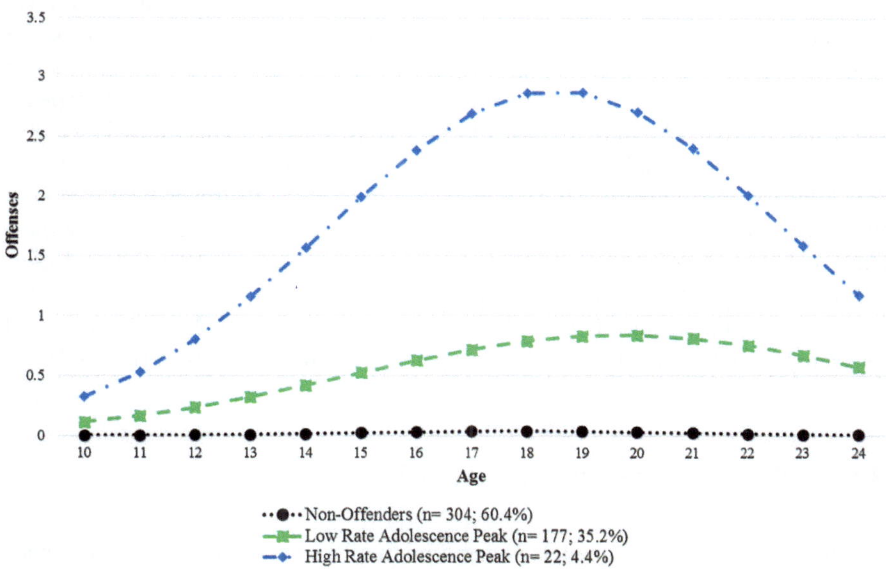

Fig. 4.3 PYS offending trajectories, ages 10–24: Youngest cohort

in the early 20s. However, the two groups differed noticeably in their rates of offending, with the low rate adolescence peak trajectory peaking at an average of one offense per year, whereas the high rate adolescence peak trajectory averaged greater than one offense per year throughout the majority of the age 10–24 time period and peaked at an average of nearly 3 offenses per year in late adolescence.

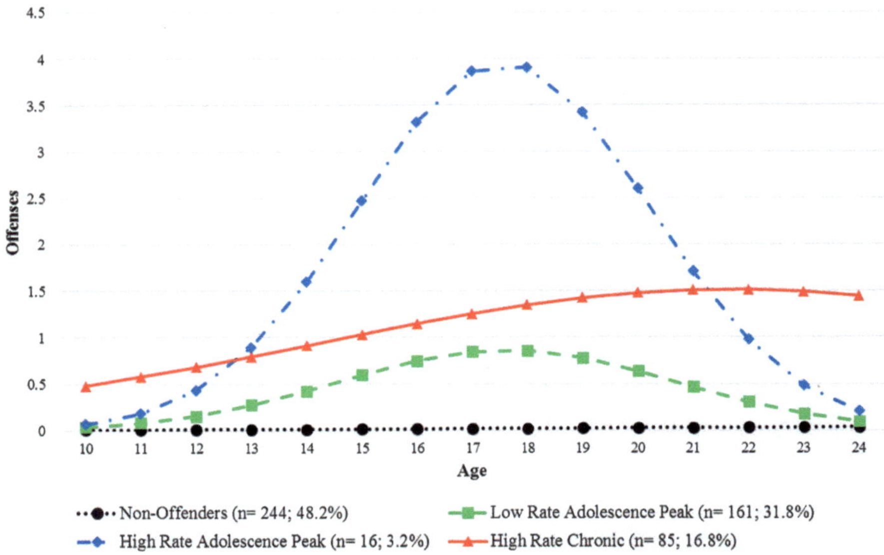

Fig. 4.4 PYS offending trajectories, ages 10–24: Oldest cohort

In contrast, four trajectory groups were identified for the Oldest cohort, with one group being a non-offender group (48.2 %). Among the three offender groups, the most prevalent was a low-rate adolescence peak trajectory (31.8 %) that began offending at ages 11–12 and steadily increased throughout adolescence before peaking at age 17/18 at an average of one offense per year and then declining in the 20s. Similarly, a high-rate adolescence peak trajectory was identified (3.2 %) that mirrored the low-rate adolescence peak trajectory in terms of its trends but differed in the average rates of offending as this trajectory considerably climbed during adolescence before peaking at nearly four offenses per year at ages 17–18 and then declining in the 20s. In addition, a high-rate chronic trajectory (16.8 %) was observed that initiated offending at age 10, steadily increased from ages 10 to 24, and maintained an average of approximately one offense per year from ages 10 to 24 (Fig. 4.4).

4.5 Offending Trajectories: Ages 10–30

The final set of trajectory models is based on the PYS participants' official offending data from ages 10 to 30. As illustrated in Fig. 4.5, four trajectories were identified for the Youngest cohort: non-offenders (50.7 %), very low-rate chronic (13.3 %), low-rate adolescence peak (31.8 %), and high-rate adolescence peak (4.2 %). Among the three offender groups, the very low-rate chronic offenders did not initiate offending until mid-adolescence, but their offending began to slowly increase in late adolescence and particularly in adulthood before reaching an average of nearly half of an offense per year by age 30. The low-rate and high-rate adolescence peak

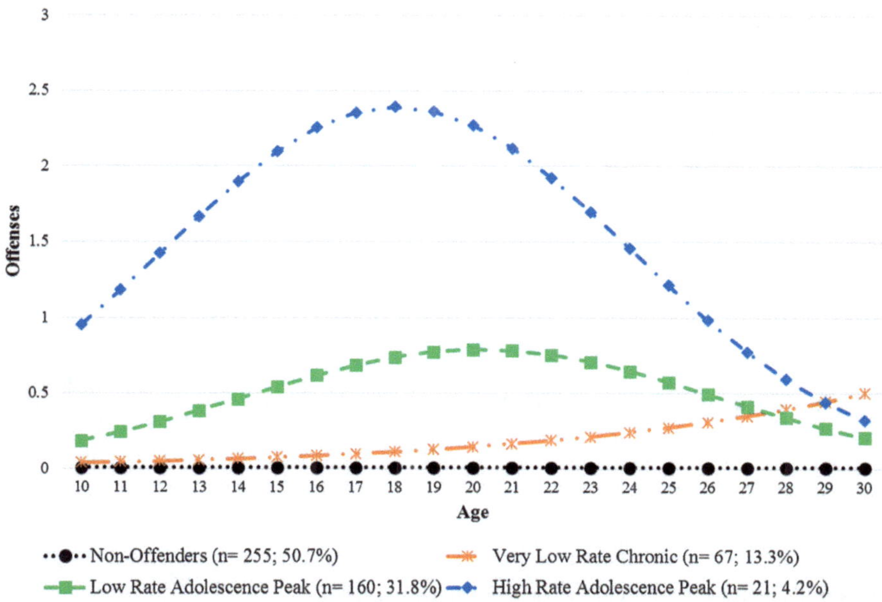

Fig. 4.5 PYS offending trajectories, ages 10–30: Youngest cohort

trajectories were similar in shape, with an onset in early adolescence, increasing in mid-to-late adolescence, peaking at age 18/19 (high adolescence peak) and age 20/21 (low-rate adolescence peak), and declining throughout the 20s. What did noticeably distinguish these two trajectories was the frequency of offending as the low-rate adolescence peak trajectory peaked at an average of one offense per year and the high-rate adolescence peak trajectory peaked averaging nearly three offenses a year.

Turning toward the ages 10–30 trajectories for the Oldest cohort, a five-trajectory solution was determined to be the best fitting model (see Fig. 4.6). The non-offender trajectory comprised approximately 47.0 % of the Oldest cohort members. Comparatively, a very low-rate chronic trajectory was observed (21.7 %), and this trajectory initiated offending at ages 11–12 and slightly increased in mid-to-late adolescence and into the early-to-mid-20s before declining in the late 20s. Although this trajectory was identifiably a chronic offending trajectory as a nonzero offending rate was observed across the entire 21 year span, the mean frequency for this trajectory remained relatively low (e.g., averaging under one offense per year). Two adolescence peak trajectories tended to mirror one another in their trends as they initiated in early adolescence, rose in frequency before peaking in mid-adolescence, and then declined in late adolescence into the 20s. The two main differences between these two trajectories were the higher offending rates observed among the high-rate adolescence peak trajectory (3.0 %) and the desistance in the mid-20s for the low-rate adolescence peak trajectory (17.4 %) compared to the high-rate adolescence peak trajectory which did not appear to reach near nonzero offending levels until

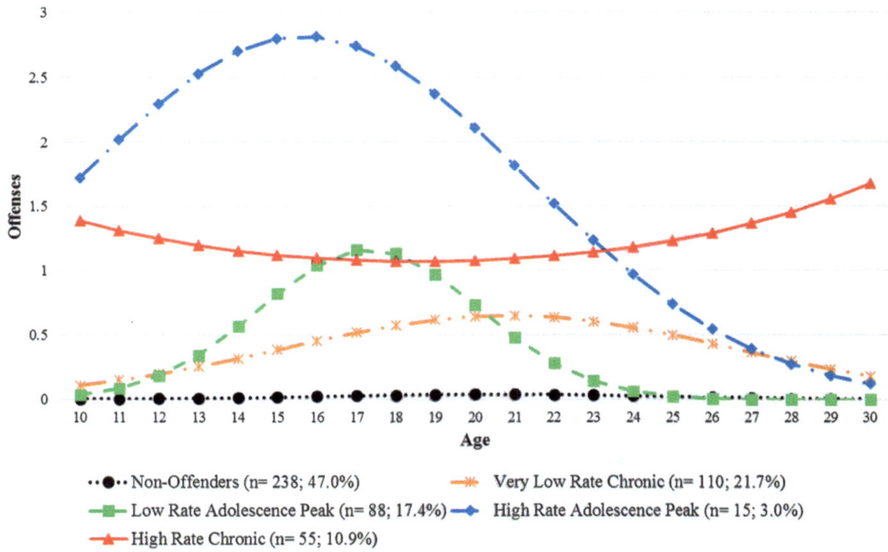

Fig. 4.6 PYS offending trajectories, ages 10–30: Oldest cohort

age 30. Finally, the high-rate chronic trajectory initiated at age 10 and maintained an average of one offense per year throughout adolescence and into the 20s before beginning to trend upward in the mid-to-late 20s to average nearly 1.5 offenses per year at age 30.[1]

4.6 Distribution of PYS Participants across Age-Band Trajectories

The final stage of the analysis in this chapter focuses on examining the distribution of the PYS participants across the various age-band trajectories and an assessment of the association between the age-band trajectories via a series of chi-square (χ^2) tests. Table 4.3 provides the results of this analysis based on a comparison of the PYS participants' ages 10–16 trajectory group assignment and their ages 10–24 and their ages 10–30 trajectory group assignment, respectively. These comparisons are

[1] It is important to note here that the PYS Oldest cohort high-rate chronic trajectory may not at first glance appear that "high rate." However, in comparison to the high-rate chronic trajectory that Farrington et al. (2013) observed in the CSDD, this PYS high-rate chronic trajectory averaged approximately one offense or greater from ages 10 to 30, whereas the CSDD high-rate chronic trajectory began averaging 0.25 offenses at age 10 and peaked at averaging one offense at age 20/21 before declining back down to an average of 0.25 offenses by age 32. Thus, while the shape/pattern of the high-rate trajectories between the CSDD and the PYS Oldest cohort may differ to some degree, both are indicative of high-rate chronic offending. In contrast, the PYS Oldest cohort high-rate chronic offenders largely offend at higher rates compared with the CSDD high-rate chronic offenders over a similarly lengthy follow-up period (ages 10–30 in the PYS; ages 10–32 in the CSDD).

Table 4.3 Ages 10–16 trajectory comparisons by cohort and trajectory assignment across age bands 10–24 and 10–30

	Youngest cohort	Youngest cohort	Youngest cohort	Oldest cohort	Oldest cohort	Oldest cohort
	Ages 10–16	Ages 10–24	Ages 10–30	Ages 10–16	Ages 10–24	Ages 10–30
Non-offenders (ages 10–16)	84.5 %	–	–	79.6 %	–	–
Non-offenders		71.3 %	60.0 %		60.5 %	59.1 %
Very low-rate chronic		–	15.5 %		–	21.8 %
Low-rate adolescence peak		27.3 %	23.3 %		29.0 %	13.4 %
High-rate adolescence peak		1.4 %	1.2 %		1.0 %	0.5 %
High-rate chronic		–	–		9.4 %	5.2 %
Adolescent onset (ages 10–16)	15.5 %	–	–	20.4 %	–	–
Non-offenders		1.3 %	0.0 %		0.0 %	0.0 %
Very low-rate chronic		–	1.3 %		–	21.4 %
Low-rate adolescence peak		78.2 %	78.2 %		42.7 %	33.0 %
High-rate adolescence peak		20.5 %	20.5 %		11.7 %	12.6 %
High-rate chronic		–	–		45.6 %	33.0 %

Note: trajectory comparisons: *ages 10–16* and ages 10–24 for Youngest cohort trajectories ($\chi^2 = 156.97$, $p < 0.001$); ages 10–30 for Youngest cohort trajectories ($\chi^2 = 178.34$, $p < 0.001$); *ages 10–16* and ages 10–24 for Oldest cohort trajectories ($\chi^2 = 160.66$, $p < 0.001$); ages 10–30 for Oldest cohort trajectories ($\chi^2 = 177.98$, $p < 0.001$)

presented by cohort. Specifically, 84.5 % of the Youngest cohort were classified as non-offenders for the ages 10–16 trajectories, and 71.3 % of these non-offenders were classified as non-offenders, 27.3 % were classified as low-rate adolescence peak, and 1.4 % were classified as high adolescence peak for the ages 10–24 trajectories. For the adolescent-onset Youngest cohort trajectory, 1.3 % of these adolescent-onset offenders at ages 10–16 were classified as non-offenders, 78.2 % were classified as low-rate adolescence peak, and 20.5 % were classified as high-rate adolescence peak for the ages 10–24 trajectories. Chi-square results revealed that there was a significant association between trajectory assignment at ages 10–16 and at ages 10–24 for the Youngest cohort ($\chi^2 = 156.97$, $p < 0.001$). Similarly, there was also a statistically significant association between trajectory assignment at ages 10–16 and ages 10–30 among the Youngest cohort ($\chi^2 = 178.34$, $p < 0.001$) as 60.0 %, 15.5 %, 23.3 %, and 1.2 % of the non-offenders at ages 10–16 were classified as non-offenders, very low-rate chronic, low-rate adolescence peak, and high-rate adolescence peak at ages 10–30 and 0.0 %, 1.3 %, 78.2 %, and 20.5 % of the Oldest cohort classified in the adolescent-onset trajectory at ages 10–16 were classified as non-offenders, very low-rate chronic, low-rate adolescence peak, and high-rate adolescence peak at ages 10–30, respectively.

Approximately 79.6 % of the Oldest cohort was classified in a non-offender trajectory at ages 10–16, and 60.5 and 59.1 % of these non-offenders were also classified as non-offenders at ages 10–24 and ages 10–30 trajectories. Furthermore, 29.0, 1.0, and 9.4 % of those classified as non-offenders at ages 10–16 were classified as low-rate adolescent peak, high-rate adolescence peak, and high-rate chronic at ages 10–24, and 21.8, 13.4, 0.5, and 5.2 % of those classified as non-offenders at ages 10–16 were classified as very low-rate chronic, low-rate adolescence peak, high-rate adolescence peak, and high-rate chronic at ages 10–30. In contrast, among the Oldest cohort participants who were classified as adolescent onset at ages 10–16, 0.0 % were classified as non-offenders at ages 10–24 and ages 10–30, 42.7 % and 33.0 % were classified as low adolescence peak at ages 10–24 and ages 10–30, 11.7 % and 12.6 % were classified as high adolescence peak at ages 10–24 and ages 10–30, 21.4 % were classified as very low-rate chronic at ages 10–30, and 45.6 % and 33.0 % were classified as high-rate chronic at ages 10–24 and 10–30, respectively. Chi-square test results revealed that the association between ages 10–16 and ages 10–24 trajectories ($\chi^2 = 160.66$, $p < 0.001$) and between the ages 10–16 and ages 10–30 trajectories ($\chi^2 = 177.98$, $p < 0.001$) was statistically significant.

Table 4.4 displays the age-band-trajectory comparisons for the ages 10–24 trajectories and the ages 10–30 trajectories for the Youngest cohort and for the Oldest cohort. For the Youngest cohort, 83.6, 15.5, 1.0, and 0.0 % of those classified as non-offenders at ages 10–24 were classified as non-offenders, very low-rate chronic, low-rate adolescence peak, and high-rate adolescence peak at ages 10–30; 0.6, 11.3, 88.1, and 0.0 % of those classified as low adolescence peak at ages 10–24 were classified as non-offenders, very low-rate chronic, low-rate adolescence peak, and high-rate adolescence peak at ages 10–30; and, 0.0, 0.0, 4.5, and 95.5 % of those classified as high adolescence peak at ages 10–24 were classified as non-offenders, very low-rate chronic, low-rate adolescence peak, and high-rate adolescence peak at ages 10–30. Concerning the Oldest cohort, 94.3, 4.5, 0.0, 0.0, and 1.2 % of those classified as non-offenders at ages 10–24 were classified as non-offenders, very low-rate chronic, low-rate ad olescence peak, high-rate adolescence peak, and high-rate chronic at ages 10–30; 5.0, 41.0, 47.2, 0.0, and 6.8 % of those classified as low-rate adolescence peak at ages 10–24 were classified as non-offenders, very low-rate chronic, low-rate adolescence peak, high-rate adolescence peak, and high-rate chronic at ages 10–30; 0.0, 0.0, 12.5, 75.0, and 12.5 % of those classified as high-rate adolescence peak at ages 10–24 were classified as non-offenders, very low-rate chronic, low-rate adolescence peak, high-rate adolescence peak, and high-rate chronic at ages 10–30; and, 0.0, 38.8, 11.8, 3.5, and 45.9 % of those classified as high-rate chronic at ages 10–24 were classified as non-offenders, very low-rate chronic, low-rate adolescence peak, high-rate adolescence peak, and high-rate chronic at ages 10–30. Chi-square tests demonstrated that these age-band-trajectory comparisons were statistically significant for the ages 10–24 and ages 10–30 trajectories and for the Youngest cohort ($\chi^2 = 899.76$, $p < 0.001$) and for the Oldest cohort ($\chi^2 = 837.29$, $p < 0.001$).

Table 4.4 Ages 10–24 trajectory comparisons by trajectory assignment across age bands 10–30

	Youngest cohort	Youngest cohort	Oldest cohort	Oldest cohort
	Ages 10–24	Ages 10–30	Ages 10–24	Ages 10–30
Non-offenders (ages 10–24)	60.4 %	–	48.2 %	–
Non-offenders		83.6 %		94.3 %
Very low-rate chronic		15.5 %		4.5 %
Low-rate adolescence peak		1.0 %		0.0 %
High-rate adolescence peak		0.0 %		0.0 %
High-rate chronic		–		1.2 %
Low adolescence peak (ages 10–24)	35.2 %	–	31.8 %	–
Non-offenders		0.6 %		5.0 %
Very low-rate chronic		11.3 %		41.0 %
Low-rate adolescence peak		88.1 %		47.2 %
High-rate adolescence peak		0.0 %		0.0 %
High-rate chronic		–		6.8 %
High adolescence peak (ages 10–24)	4.4 %	–	3.2 %	–
Non-offenders		0.0 %		0.0 %
Very low-rate chronic		0.0 %		0.0 %
Low-rate adolescence peak		4.5 %		12.5 %
High-rate adolescence peak		95.5 %		75.0 %
High-rate chronic		–		12.5 %
High-rate chronic (ages 10–24)	–	–	16.8 %	–
Non-offenders				0.0 %
Very low-rate chronic				38.8 %
Low-rate adolescence peak				11.8 %
High-rate adolescence peak				3.5 %
High-rate chronic				45.9 %

Note: trajectory comparisons: *ages 10–24* and ages 10–30 for Youngest cohort trajectories ($\chi^2 = 899.76$, $p < 0.001$); *ages 10–24* and ages 10–30 for Oldest cohort trajectories ($\chi^2 = 837.29$, $p < 0.001$)

4.7 Summary

This chapter provided an estimation of a series of group-based trajectories of offending across three age bands (e.g., ages 10–16, ages 10–24, and ages 10–30) to (1) determine the appropriate number and shape of potentially important subgroup offending patterns, to (2) assess the age/time period where trajectories appear to crystallize, and to (3) evaluate the association between age-band-trajectory group assignments. All of the analyses were performed for the Youngest and Oldest cohorts, separately. Among the Youngest cohort, the results identified two trajectory groups for ages 10–16 (non-offenders and adolescent-onset offenders), three trajectory groups for ages 10–24 (non-offenders, low-rate adolescence peak, and high-rate adolescence peak), and four trajectory groups for ages 10–30 (non-offenders, very low-rate chronic, low-rate adolescence peak, and high-rate adolescence peak). Comparatively, among the Oldest cohort, two trajectory groups were identified for ages 10–16 (non-offenders and adolescent-onset offenders), four trajectory groups for ages 10–24 (non-offenders, low-rate adolescence peak, high-rate adolescence peak, and high-rate chronic), and five trajectory groups for ages 10–30 (non-offenders, very low-rate chronic, low-rate adolescence peak, high-rate adolescence peak, and high-rate chronic). Additional chi-square test (χ^2) comparisons revealed that there were significant associations between the age-band-trajectory group assignments, with most of the PYS participants being assigned as non-offenders at the ages 10–16 age-band trajectory also being assigned as non-offenders in the subsequent age-band trajectories, for example. Alternatively, when there was trajectory group "switching" observed across the age bands, it was most notably due to non-offenders at ages 10–16 becoming active in adulthood or offenders escalating, de-escalating, or desisting their offending in subsequent age bands, resulting in them being reassigned to a group-based trajectory that better approximated their longer-term offending patterns. By and large, the number and shape of the trajectory groups appeared to crystallize at ages 10–30, and these results in general were observed in both PYS cohorts.

Chapter 5
Conclusions

5.1 Official Offending

With respect to official offending, our analyses found that 42.4 % of the Youngest cohort and 50.1 % of the Oldest cohort were convicted at least once for either moderate theft, serious theft, moderate violence, serious violence, or drug dealing up to age 30, and the Youngest and Oldest cohorts accumulated 1080 and 1437 offenses in total by age 30, respectively. Furthermore, robust evidence was discovered regarding the continuity in official offending over various age bands (e.g., ages 10–14, ages 15–18, ages 19–24, and ages 25–30), as the Odds Ratios for the comparisons of whether or not the PYS participant was convicted in one particular age band relative to another (all of which were statistically significant) ranged from 3.5 to 8.5 and 4.2 to 7.2 for the Youngest and Oldest cohorts, respectively.

For the Youngest cohort, the criminal career length ranged from 0.81 years for those who did not initiate offending until ages 25–30 to 9.99 years for those who initiated offending during ages 10–14. The longest criminal career length, 11.58 years, was observed for the most frequent offenders (15+ convictions). The average age of onset also ranged from 13.04 (among those who initiated at ages 10–14) to 27.10 (among those who initiated at ages 25–30). In contrast, among the Oldest cohort, the age of onset ranged from an average of 13.34 (among those who initiated at ages 10–14) to an average of 27.09 (among those who initiated at ages 25–30), with the longest criminal career (11.40 years) being observed for those offenders with 15+ convictions. Other criminal career information for the Youngest cohort revealed that 33.7 % were convicted by age 20 and 28.7 % were convicted between ages 21–30, and among the offenders, 80.5 % were recidivists, 42.9 % were chronic offenders (5+ convictions), and 7.8 % had a criminal career of 15+ years, whereas 42.1 % were convicted by age 20 and 27.5 % were convicted between ages 21–30, and among the offenders, 75.0 % were recidivists, 43.9 % were chronic offenders (5+ convictions), and 5.3 % had a criminal career of 15+ years among the Oldest cohort.

© The Authors 2016

W.G. Jennings et al., *Offending from Childhood to Young Adulthood*,
SpringerBriefs in Criminology, DOI 10.1007/978-3-319-25966-6_5

With this descriptive information in hand, it is important to briefly mention a few noteworthy similarities and differences between the two PYS cohorts in terms of their officially recorded offending. For example, the prevalence of offending is substantively greater overall (ages 10–30) and for ages 15–18 and ages 19–24 in particular for the Oldest cohort, whereas the prevalence estimates were nearly equivalent for the two cohorts at ages 10–14 and ages 25–30. Second, moderate theft was the most prevalent crime committed by both cohorts. Third, more participants in the Oldest cohort were active in serious theft and violence at ages 15–18 and ages 19–24 and were active in drug dealing at ages 15–18, 19–24, and 25–30 compared with the Youngest cohort. Finally, many more of the Oldest cohort participants were involved in moderate and serious theft relative to the Youngest cohort over ages 10–30, although their prevalence of officially recorded involvement in moderate and serious violence over ages 10–30 is comparable.

The PYS analyses were largely modeled on similar analyses using data from the CSDD and offer a unique insight in onset, continuity, and trajectories between the two studies. Such systematic comparisons are very rare among longitudinal studies (e.g., Loeber et al. 1999; Farrington and Loeber 1999). Before reporting the comparisons between the two studies, it should be stressed that both studies started in childhood, concerned inner-city samples of young males (London, Great Britain, and Pittsburgh, Pennsylvania, United States), and had regular follow-up assessments over more than two decades which included official records of delinquency, complemented by self-reported delinquency. However, some notable differences between the studies should also be mentioned. The CSDD started in a different era than the PYS, the justice system response to delinquents in London and Pittsburgh only partly overlap, and the timing and format of self-reported delinquency were not exactly the same. Despite these differences, it is still worthwhile to compare the delinquency career results of the male participants in the two studies.

As illustrated in Table 5.1, there are a number of important similarities and differences between the official delinquency records based on the CSDD and the official delinquency records based on the PYS Youngest and Oldest cohorts. First, the overall prevalence of offending was substantially lower for the CSDD (29.3 %, ages 10–47) compared to 42.4 % and 50.1 % for the PYS Youngest and Oldest cohorts (ages 10–30), respectively, even though the follow-up for the CSDD was much longer. Second, the age-band-specific prevalence estimates were also comparable as well. For example, 10.5 % of the CSDD males, 14.5 % of PYS Youngest cohort, and 14.6 % of the PYS Oldest cohort had at least one officially recorded offense at ages 10–14. Third, the prevalence of offending was highest at ages 15–18 for the CSDD (19.0 %) and the PYS Oldest cohort (34.0 %) participants and highest at ages 19–24 for the PYS Youngest cohort (26.5 %). Fourth, prevalence estimates for ages 27–32 for the CSDD participants were 9.3 % and approximately 16.0 % for the PYS Youngest and Oldest cohort at ages 25–30. Finally, several other noteworthy similarities were observed for the continuity in offending over age (CSDD Odds Ratios ranged from 1.9 to 26.6; PYS Youngest cohort Odds Ratios ranged from 3.5 to 8.5; PYS Oldest cohort Odds Ratios ranged from 4.2 to 7.2), the average number of

Table 5.1 Official offending comparisons between the CSDD and the PYS Youngest and Oldest cohorts

	CSDD (n=404)	PYS Youngest cohort (n=503)	PYS Oldest cohort (n=506)
	Ages 10–47	Ages 10–30	Ages 10–30
Prevalence of offenders			
Age 10–14	10.5 %	14.5 %	14.6 %
Age 15–18	19.0 %	24.4 %	34.0 %
Age 19–24	–	26.5 %	31.4 %
Age 25–30 (age 27–32 in CSDD)	9.3 %	16.7 %	16.0 %
Age 42–47	4.7 %	–	–
All ages	29.3 %	42.4 %	50.1 %
Cumulative no. of offenses	829	1080	1437
Average no. offenses	4.90	5.27	5.89
Continuity in offending (ORs)	1.9–26.6	3.5–8.5	4.2–7.2
Average career length	9.80	5.62	4.87
Most prevalent offense	Burglary	Moderate theft	Moderate theft
% recidivist offenders	70.0 %	80.5 %	75.0 %
Offenders with 15+ offenses			
Prevalence	7.6 %	5.9 %	8.2 %
Average age at first offense	13.2	13.50	13.75
Average age at last offense	38.5	25.08	25.15
Average career length	25.3	11.58	11.40

Note: CSDD=Cambridge Study in Delinquent Development, PYS=Pittsburgh Youth Study, ORs=Odds Ratios. CSDD estimates based on burglary, theft of vehicle, theft from vehicle, shoplifting, theft from machine, theft from work, other theft, receiving stolen goods, suspected persons, robbery, assault, threats, offensive weapon possession, and vandalism offenses. PYS estimates based on moderate theft (stealing a bicycle or skateboard from the street, stealing things worth more than $5, joyriding, purse snatching, dealing in stolen goods, or stealing from a car), serious theft (breaking-and-entering or auto theft), moderate violence (gang fighting), serious violence (forcible robbery, attacking with intent to injure, sexual coercion, or rape), and drug dealing (selling of marijuana or hard drugs) offenses.

offenses (CSDD=4.90; PYS Youngest cohort=5.27; PYS Oldest cohort=5.89), the percentage of offenders who were recidivists (70.0–80.5 %), and the prevalence of severely chronic offenders who had 15+ offenses (5.9–8.2 %).

5.2 Self-Reported Offending

Turning toward self-reported offending, our analyses found that the prevalence of moderate and serious self-reported offending was 56.3 % for the Youngest cohort and 76.5 % for the Oldest cohort up to age 30. Similar to what was observed in the official offending data, there was a considerable amount of evidence demonstrating continuity in self-reported offending as well, as the Odds Ratios for the comparisons of whether or not the PYS participant self-reported offending in one particular age band relative to another (all of which were statistically significant) ranged from 2.5 to 9.7 and 1.1–6.4 for the Youngest and Oldest cohorts, respectively. After scaling up the official offending estimates based on self-reported offending estimates, the corresponding self-reported-to-official-offending ratios ranged from 3.43 for serious violence offenses to 290.25 for drug dealing offenses and 105.10 overall for the Youngest cohort, compared to a range of 2.95 for serious violence offenses to 327.73 for drug dealing offenses and 130.24 overall for the Oldest cohort. Overall, the self-reported-to-official-offending ratio for only those PYS participants who were convicted was 76.01 and 102.96 for the Youngest and Oldest cohorts, respectively.

Turning toward a more detailed comparison between the two PYS cohorts, the prevalence of self-reported offending at ages 10–30 was much greater for the Oldest cohort compared with the Youngest cohort. Furthermore, while the prevalence of self-reported offending was fairly similar at ages 10–14 for both cohorts, the prevalence of offending for the Oldest cohort compared with the Youngest cohort was nearly two to three times greater at ages 15–18 and ages 19–24, respectively. Similar to what was observed for the officially recorded crime, moderate theft was the most prevalent form of self-reported offending for both cohorts. Regarding crime-specific prevalence estimates, more participants in the Oldest cohort were active in moderate and serious violence and drug dealing relative to the Youngest cohort at ages 15–18 and 19–24. Finally, the Oldest cohort was markedly more active in all types of crime compared to the Youngest cohort at ages 19–24 in particular.

Table 5.2 provides a series of self-report offending comparisons between the CSDD and the PYS Youngest and Oldest cohorts. For example, the self-reported prevalence of offending was greater than 50 % for the CSDD participants and both PYS cohorts, with the estimates ranging from 56.3 % (Youngest PYS cohort, ages 10–30) and 76.5 % (Oldest PYS cohort, ages 10–30) to 93.3 % (CSDD, ages 10–47). For the comparable age categories between the CSDD and the PYS, age-band-specific prevalence rates for self-reported offending ranged from 47.4 % (ages 27–32) to 77.8 % (ages 10–14) for the CSDD, 19.4 % (ages 19–24 and ages 25–30) to 41.1 % (ages 10–14) for the Youngest PYS cohort, and 6.8 % (ages 25–30) to 64.0 % (ages 15–18) for the Oldest PYS cohort. Furthermore, vandalism was the most prevalent offense for the CSDD participants, and theft was the most prevalent offense for both PYS cohorts. Similar to what was observed for the official data discussed above, there was considerable and comparable continuity in offending observed over age for the CSDD (ORs = 1.7–5.3) and the PYS Youngest (ORs = 2.5–9.7) and Oldest cohorts (ORs = 1.1–6.4). Finally, self-report-to-official-offending ratios ranged from 14.64 (PYS Youngest cohort) to 22.40 (PYS Oldest cohort) to 38.70 (CSDD) and 10.66 (PYS Youngest cohort) to 16.28 (PYS Oldest cohort) to 21.70 (CSDD) when focusing only on those individuals who had been convicted. In other words, for every one officially recoded offense, the CSDD and the PYS males self-reported committing approximately 15–39 offenses in general or approximately 11–22 offenses specifically among the CSDD and PYS males who were convicted.

Table 5.2 Self-report offending comparisons between the CSDD and the PYS Youngest and Oldest cohorts

	CSDD (n=404)	PYS Youngest cohort (n=503)	PYS Oldest cohort (n=506)
	Ages 10–47	Ages 10–30	Ages 10–30
Prevalence of offenders			
Ages 10–14	77.8 %	41.1 %	47.4 %
Ages 15–18	76.3 %	36.1 %	64.0 %
Ages 19–24	–	19.4 %	56.0 %
Ages 25–30 (ages 27–32 in CSDD)	47.4 %	19.4 %	6.8 %
Ages 42–47	27.9 %	–	–
All Ages	93.3 %	56.3 %	76.5 %
Most prevalent offense	Vandalism	Moderate theft	Moderate theft
Continuity in offending (ORs)	1.7–5.3	2.5–9.7	1.1–6.4
Self-report-to-official-offending ratio	38.70	14.64	22.40
Self-report-to-official-offending ratio (convicted offenders only)	21.70	10.66	16.28

Note: CSDD=Cambridge Study in Delinquent Development, PYS=Pittsburgh Youth Study, ORs=Odds Ratios. CSDD estimates based on burglary, theft of vehicle, theft from vehicle, shoplifting, theft from machine, assault, drug use, and vandalism offenses. PYS estimates based on moderate theft (stealing a bicycle or skateboard from the street, stealing things worth more than $5, joyriding, purse snatching, dealing in stolen goods, or stealing from a car), serious theft (breaking-and-entering or auto theft), moderate violence (gang fighting), and serious violence (forcible robbery, attacking with intent to injure, sexual coercion, or rape) offenses.

5.3 Trajectories of Offending

Taken together, three age-band trajectories were estimated separately for the Youngest and Oldest cohorts based on their official offending at ages 10–16, ages 10–24, and ages 10–30. Our trajectory analyses revealed two trajectories of offending for ages 10–16 (non-offenders = 84.5 % and adolescent onset = 15.5 %), three offending trajectories at age 10–24 (non-offenders = 60.4 %, low-rate adolescence peak = 35.2 %, and high-rate adolescence peak = 4.4 %), and four offending trajectories at ages 10–30 (non-offenders = 50.7 %, very low-rate chronic = 13.3 %, low-rate adolescence peak = 31.8 %, and high-rate adolescence peak = 4.2 %) for the Youngest cohort. Comparatively, two trajectories of offending were identified for the Oldest cohort at ages 10–16 (non-offenders = 79.6 % and adolescent onset = 20.4 %), four trajectories at ages 10–24 (non-offenders = 48.2 %, low-rate adolescence peak = 31.8 %, high-rate adolescence peak = 3.2 %, and high-rate chronic = 16.8 %), and five trajectories at ages 10–30 (non-offenders = 47.0 %, very low-rate chronic = 21.7 %, low-rate adolescence peak = 17.4 %, high-rate adolescence peak = 3.0 %, and high-rate chronic = 10.9 %).

Generally speaking, these analyses from both PYS cohorts suggest that the number and shape of the trajectories began to crystallize by ages 10–24 and certainly by ages 10–30, and additional chi-square test (χ^2) comparisons revealed that there were significant associations between the age-band-trajectory group assignments. In other words, trajectory group assignment in one age band was associated with trajectory group assignment in the subsequent age band(s). When "shifting" occurred in trajectory group assignment, it was primarily due to individuals becoming active, becoming inactive, or increasing or decreasing their offense frequency at certain ages, thus upgrading (e.g., low-rate adolescent peak to high-rate adolescence peak) or downgrading (e.g., high-rate adolescence peak to low-rate adolescence peak) their trajectory group assignment.

Table 5.3 compares the offending trajectory groups by comparable age bands for the CSDD and the PYS participants. The ages 10–16 age-band trajectories revealed the same number and type of trajectory groups in the two studies, e.g., non-offenders and adolescent-onset offenders. Across the two studies, the prevalence of these trajectory groups ranged from 79.6 to 91.8 % for the non-offenders and 8.2–20.4 % for the adolescent-onset offenders. The ages 10–24 trajectories identified four distinct trajectory groups for the CSDD participants (non-offenders = 77.5 %, very low-rate chronic = 7.2 %, low-rate adolescence peak = 9.7 %, high-rate adolescence peak = 5.7 %) and for the PYS Oldest cohort (non-offenders = 48.2 %, low-rate adolescence peak = 31.8 %, high-rate adolescence peak = 3.2 %, high-rate chronic = 16.8 %) and three distinct trajectory groups for the PYS Youngest cohort (non-offenders = 60.4 %, low-rate adolescence peak = 35.2 %, high-rate adolescence peak = 4.4 %). Finally, the ages 10–32 trajectories for the CSDD participants yielded five distinct trajectory groups including non-offenders (67.1 %), very low-rate chronic (11.1 %), low-rate adolescence peak (15.8 %), high-rate adolescence peak (3.5 %), and high-rate chronic (2.5 %). Comparatively, this same number and type of trajectory groups were identified for the PYS Oldest cohort for the ages 10–30 trajectories with the non-offenders comprising 47.0 % of the sample, followed by very low-rate chronic (21.7 %), low-rate adolescence peak (17.4 %), high-rate adolescence peak (3.0 %), and high-rate chronic (10.9 %). In comparison four trajectory groups were identified for the PYS Youngest cohort (non-offenders = 50.7 %, very low-rate chronic = 13.3 %, low-rate adolescence peak = 31.8 %, high-rate adolescence peak = 4.2 %).

In conclusion, the trajectory analyses comparisons for the CSDD and the PYS cohorts paint a remarkably similar story with regard to (1) the number of trajectory groups (2 at ages 10–16; 3–4 at ages 10–24; 4–5 at ages 10–30/32), (2) the shape of the trajectory groups (non-offenders, adolescent onset, very low-rate chronic, low-rate adolescence peak, high-rate adolescence peak, and high-rate chronic), and (3) the age band in which the trajectories appear to begin to crystallize (ages 10–30/32). Additionally, the prevalence of the trajectory groups is largely similar when comparing the CSDD and the PYS cohorts as the non-offenders comprise the largest trajectory group, followed by the low-rate adolescence peak and the very low-rate chronic. In contrast, the high-rate adolescence peak and the high-rate chronic trajectories comprise the fewest number of CSDD and PYS cohort males, specifically.

Table 5.3 Offending trajectory group comparisons by age bands between the CSDD (ages 10–16, ages 10–24, ages 10–32) and the PYS Youngest and Oldest cohorts (ages 10–16, ages 10–24, ages 10–30)

	CSDD	PYS Youngest cohort	PYS Oldest cohort	CSDD	PYS Youngest cohort	PYS Oldest cohort	CSDD	PYS Youngest cohort	PYS Oldest cohort
	Ages 10–16	Ages 10–16	Ages 10–16	Ages 10–24	Ages 10–24	Ages 10–24	Ages 10–32	Ages 10–30	Ages 10–30
Non-offenders	91.8 %	84.5 %	79.6 %	77.5 %	60.4 %	48.2 %	67.1 %	50.7 %	47.0 %
Adolescent onset	8.2 %	15.5 %	20.4 %		–	–		–	–
Very low-rate chronic	–	–	–	7.2 %	–	–	11.1 %	13.3 %	21.7 %
Low-rate adolescence peak	–	–	–	9.7 %	35.2 %	31.8 %	15.8 %	31.8 %	17.4 %
High-rate adolescence peak	–	–	–	5.7 %	4.4 %	3.2 %	3.5 %	4.2 %	3.0 %
High-rate chronic	–	–	–	–	–	16.8 %	2.5 %	–	10.9 %
Total	100.0 %	100.0 %	100.0 %	100.0 %	100.0 %	100.0 %	100.0 %	100.0 %	100.0 %

Note: CSDD = Cambridge Study in Delinquent Development, PYS = Pittsburgh Youth Study.

5.4 Theoretical Implications

The main theoretical implications that can be drawn from our results are that there is noticeable continuity in offending, and this continuity is documented in official offending records and in self-reports. In this same vein, there are also individuals who do not show this continuity and may be active or inactive in a particular age band(s) over the life-course. Relatedly, many offenders are recidivists and others are not, some offenders have a very early age of onset and others do not commit their first offense until adulthood, and some offenders have a relatively brief criminal career whereas others display considerable chronicity and exhibit very lengthy criminal careers. Another interesting and important contribution of our book toward criminological theorizing concerns the implications of scaling up official records based on self-reported offending. Specifically, these findings revealed that there many more self-reported offenders relative to those that are documented as for every one officially recorded offense the PYS cohort participants self-report committing approximately 15–23 offenses. Therefore, criminological theorizing and theory testing that is narrowly focused on official records of offending alone and not based on scaled up offending estimates informed by self-reports are limited in scope and may lead to biased theoretical assumptions. In addition, this narrow focus may also result in inaccuracies in determining the levels of empirical support for certain theoretical perspectives and in assessing certain criminal career dimensions such as age of onset, offending frequency, chronic offending, career length, etc.

In addition, the group-based trajectory results have identified a number of unique trajectory groups that emerge depending on the length of follow-up, including: non-offenders, very low-rate chronic, low-rate adolescence peak, high-rate adolescence peak, and high-rate chronic. Not only are these trajectories similar in number and shape to the majority of those reported in prior trajectory-based research with a similarly lengthy follow-up period (Farrington et al. 2013; Jennings and Reingle 2012; Piquero 2008) but they too suggest the potential need for risk and protective factor analyses to assess which theoretical frameworks and which set(s) or domain(s) of risk and protective factors may be relevant for distinguishing these group-based trajectories. These types of analyses can inform the theoretical literature by providing support for either general theories of crime or for more developmentally informed age-graded theories of crime. Future research is encouraged to embark on this important research agenda (e.g., see Jennings et al. 2010; Maldonado-Molina et al. 2009). In sum, all of these analyses and criminal career offending dimensions would seem to point toward a middle-ground theoretical perspective (Brame et al. 2003) rather than solely a persistent heterogeneity or state dependence theoretical framework (Nagin and Paternoster 1991; Nagin and Farrington 1992) for explaining offending over the life-course.

5.5 Policy Implications

Specifically, when considering the results from the PYS and the CSDD together, the officially recorded estimates of offending at ages 10–30 suggest that (1) the prevalence of offending is approximately 30–50 %, (2) the offenders commit roughly 5 offenses on average and 800–1400 offenses cumulatively, (3) property theft is the most prevalent form of offending, (4) there is identifiable continuity in offending over age, and (5) nearly three out of every four offenders re-offend. Furthermore, the self-reported estimates of offending reveal that (1) the prevalence of offending is greater than 50 % up to nearly 100 %, (2) property theft is the most prevalent offense, (3) there is documented continuity in offending over age, and (4) there are as many as 39 offenses self-reported for every one officially recorded offense. Therefore, the primary implications from our results and our replication in the PYS of many of the analyses documented in the CSDD (Farrington et al. 2013) are that the focus and effort should be directed toward early prevention and intervention.

This evidence coupled with the fact that many of the CSDD and the PYS cohort participants began offending at an early age, many continued this behavior up to age 30, and many also escalated in terms of their frequency as they aged suggests that in order to provide the "best bang for the buck," early life-course intervention in general and targeting chronic offenders specifically are paramount. Once a criminal career has been initiated and offending begins to increase in terms of frequency and escalate in terms of seriousness, the probability of rehabilitation diminishes, whereas the financial toll on society grows exponentially (see Cohen and Piquero 2009). In addition, as property offending (burglary, theft, vandalism, etc.) was the most prevalent form of offending identified in the PYS and in the CSDD, it would seem plausible that interventions targeting the prevention of this crime such as crime prevention through environmental design (Clarke and Felson 2011; Newman 1972) or hot spots policing may seem fruitful. Also, as the overwhelming majority of offenders were determined to be recidivists, intervention programs should be designed with evidence-based principles aimed at reducing recidivism and promoting more effective rehabilitation and reentry (Sherman et al. 1998).

Also, further early life-course policy and prevention efforts should be initiated that have been demonstrated to be effective such as cognitive behavioral therapy (Landenberger and Lipsey 2005), child skills training (Hawkins et al. 2005), and self-control modification programs (Piquero et al. 2010). Furthermore, Piquero et al. (2009) have recently documented the considerable success of early family/parent training programs and nurse home visitation programs for reducing conduct problems, delinquency, and a multitude of later-life adverse outcomes. In this vein, Cohen et al. (2010a) have also revealed that programs such as these are cost effective as well. Ultimately, given the magnitude of the personal, social, and economic costs of a life-course of offending and how these costs are differentially distributed and borne across offender trajectories (Cohen et al. 2010b, c; Piquero et al. 2013), such as those trajectories identified in the CSDD (Farrington et al. 2013) and largely replicated here in the PYS, it is imperative that investments be made in early life-course prevention and intervention to alter the shape of these trajectories and to promote desistance.

Appendix: Pittsburgh Youth Study Publications (Books, Peer-Reviewed Papers, and Chapters)

Books

Boots, D. P. (2008). *Mental health and violent youth. A developmental/lifecourse perspective*. New York: LFB Scholarly Publishing LLC (published dissertation).

Loeber, R., & Farrington, D. P. (2011). *Young homicide offenders and victims: Development, risk factors and prediction from childhood*. New York: Springer.

Loeber, R., Farrington, D. P., Stouthamer-Loeber, M., & Van Kammen, W. B. (1998). *Antisocial behavior and mental health problems: Explanatory factors in childhood and adolescence*. Mahwah, NJ: Lawrence Erlbaum.

Loeber, R., Farrington, D. P., Stouthamer-Loeber, M., & White, H. R. (2008). *Violence and serious theft: Development and prediction from childhood to adulthood*. New York: Routledge.

Murray, J., Bijleveld, C. C. J. H., Farrington, D. P., & Loeber, R. (2014). *Effects of parental incarceration on children: Cross-national comparative studies*. Washington, DC: American Psychological Association Press.

Stouthamer-Loeber, M., & Van Kammen, W. B. (1995). *Data collection and management: A practical guide*. Newbury Park, CA: Sage.

Peer-Reviewed Papers

Ahonen, A., Loeber, R., & Pardini, D. (in press). The prediction of young homicide and violent offenders. *Justice Quarterly* .http://www.tandfonline.com/doi/abs/10.1080/07418825.2015.1081263#.VlxbDNKrSkI.

Angold, A., Erkanli, A., Loeber, R., Costello, E. J., Van Kammen, W. B., & Stouthamer-Loeber, M. (1996). Disappearing depression in a population sample of boys. *Journal of Emotional & Behavioral Disorders, 4*, 95–104.

Averdijk, M., & Loeber, R. (2012). The role of self-control in the link between prior and future victimisation: an indirect test. *International Review of Victimology, 18*, 189–206.

Bechtold, J., Simpson, T., White, H., & Pardini, D. A. (2015). Chronic adolescent marijuana use as a risk factor for physical and mental health problems in young adult men. *Psychology of Addictive Behaviors, 29*, 552.

© The Authors 2016

W.G. Jennings et al., *Offending from Childhood to Young Adulthood*,
SpringerBriefs in Criminology, DOI 10.1007/978-3-319-25966-6

Berg, M. T., & Loeber, R. (2011). Examining the neighborhood context of the violent offending-victimization relationship: A prospective investigation. *Journal of Quantitative Criminology, 27*, 427–451.

Berg, M. T., Slocum, L. A., & Loeber, R. (2013). Illegal behavior, neighborhood context, and police reporting by victims of violence. *Journal of Research in Crime and Delinquency, 50*, 75–103.

Beyers, J. M., Loeber, R., Wikström, P. O., & Stouthamer-Loeber, M. (2001). What predicts adolescent violence in better-off neighborhoods? *Journal of Abnormal Child Psychology, 29*, 369–381.

Browning, K., Huizinga, D., Loeber, R., & Thornberry, T. P. (1999, April). Causes and Correlates of Delinquency Program. OJJDP Fact Sheet.

Browning, K., & Loeber, R. (1999, February). Highlights of findings from the Pittsburgh Youth Study. OJJDP Fact Sheet, No. 95.

Burke, J. D., Loeber, R., White, H. R., Stouthamer-Loeber, M., & Pardini, D. A. (2007). Inattention as a key predictor of tobacco use in adolescence. *Journal of Abnormal Psychology, 116*, 249–259.

Byrd, A. L., Loeber, R., & Pardini, D. A. (2012). Understanding desisting and persisting forms of delinquency: The unique contributions of disruptive behavior disorders and interpersonal callousness. *Journal of Child Psychology and Psychiatry, 53*, 371–380.

Caspi, A., Moffitt, T. E., Silva, P. A., Stouthamer-Loeber, M., Krueger, R. F., & Schmutte, P. S. (1994). Are some people crime prone? Replications of the personality-crime relationship across countries, genders, races, and methods. *Criminology, 32*, 163–195.

Cerda, M., Bordelois, P. M., Keyes, K. M., Galea, S., Koenen, K. C., & Pardini, D. (2013). Cumulative and recent psychiatric symptoms as predictors of substance use onset: does timing matter? *Addiction, 108*, 2119–2128.

Colins, O., Andershed, H., & Pardini, D. (in press). Psychopathic traits as a predictor of future criminality, intimate partner aggression and substance use in young men. *Law and Human Behavior*. http://www.ncbi.nlm.nih.gov/pubmed/26301710.

Copas, J., & Loeber, R. (1990). Relative improvement over chance for 2 x 2 tables. *British Journal of Statistical and Mathematical Psychology, 43*, 293–307.

Cronley, C., White, H. R., Mun, E. Y., Lee, C., Finlay, A., & Loeber, R. (2012). Exploring the interaction effect of neighborhood racial composition and individual race on substance use among male adolescents. *Journal of Ethnicity in Substance Abuse, 11*, 52–74.

Defoe, I. N., Farrington, D. P., & Loeber, R. (2013). Disentangling the relationship between delinquency and hyperactivity, low achievement, depression, and low socioeconomic status: Analysis of repeated longitudinal data. *Journal of Criminal Justice, 41*, 100–107.

Duckworth, A. L., Quinn, P. D., Lynam, D. R., Loeber, R., & Stouthamer-Loeber, M. (2011). Role of test motivation in intelligence testing. *PNAS, 108*, 7716–7720.

Fabio, A., Loeber, R., Balasurbramani, G. K., Roth, J., & Farrington, D. P. (2006). Why some generations are more violent than others: Assessment of age, period, and cohort effects. *American Journal of Epidemiology, 164*, 151–160.

Fabio, A., Tu, L., Loeber, R., & Cohen, J. (2011). Neighborhood socioeconomic disadvantage and the shape of the age-crime curve. *American Journal of Public Health, 101*, S325–S332.

Fabio, A., Yan, Z., Wisniewski, S. R., Henry, D. B., Farrington, D. P., Bridge, J. A., et al. (2008). Cohort differences in the progression of developmental pathways: Evidence for period effects on secular trends of violence in males. *Injury Prevention, 14*, 311–318.

Fabrega, H., Ulrich, R., & Loeber, R. (1996). Adolescent psychopathology as a function of informant and risk status. *Journal of Nervous and Mental Diseases, 184*, 27–34.

Farrington, D. P., Jolliffe, D., Loeber, R., Stouthamer-Loeber, M., & Kalb, L. (2001). The concentration of offenders in families, and family criminality in the prediction of boys' delinquency. *Journal of Adolescence, 24*, 579–596.

Farrington, D. P., Jolliffe, D., Loeber, R., & Homish, D. L. (2007). How many offenses are really committed per juvenile court offender? *Victims and Offenders, 2*, 227–249.

Farrington, D., & Loeber, R. (1989). RIOC and Phi as measures of predictive efficiency and strength of association in 2 x 2 tables. *Journal of Quantitative Criminology, 5*, 201–213.

Farrington, D. P., & Loeber, R. (1999). Risk factors for delinquency over time and place. *Youth Update, 17*(2), 4–5.

Farrington, D. P., & Loeber, R. (2000). Some benefits of dichotomization in psychiatric and criminological research. *Criminal Behaviour and Mental Health, 10*, 102–122.

Farrington, D. P., Loeber, R., Stallings, R., & Ttofi, M. (2011). Bullying perpetration and victimization as predictors of delinquency and depression in the Pittsburgh Youth Study. *Journal of Aggression, Conflict and Peace Research, 3*, 74–81.

Farrington, D. P., Loeber, R., Stouthamer-Loeber, M., Van Kammen, W. B., & Schmidt, L. (1996). Self-reported delinquency and a combined delinquency seriousness scale based on boys, mothers, and teachers: Concurrent and predictive validity for African-Americans and Caucasians. *Criminology, 34*, 493–517.

Farrington, D. P., Loeber, R., Yin, Y., & Anderson, S. (2002). Are within-individual causes of delinquency the same as between-individual causes? *Criminal Behaviour and Mental Health, 12*, 53–68.

Farrington, D. P., Loeber, R., & Berg, M. (2012). Young men who kill: A prospective longitudinal examination from childhood. *Homicide Studies, 16*, 99–128.

Fite, P. J., Raine, A., Stouthamer-Loeber, M., Loeber, R., & Pardini, D. A. (2009). Reactive and proactive aggression in adolescent males: Examining differential outcomes 10-years later in early adulthood. *Criminal Justice and Behavior, 37*, 141–157.

Fite, P. J., Rubens, S. L., Preddy, T. M., Raine, A., & Pardini, D. A. (2014). Reactive/proactive aggression and the development of internalizing problems in males: The moderating effect of parent and peer relationships. *Aggressive Behavior, 40*(1), 69–78.

Fite, P. J., Wynn, P., & Pardini, D. A. (2009). Explaining discrepancies between African-American and Caucasian juvenile arrest rates in males. *Journal of Consulting and Clinical Psychology, 77*, 916–927.

Frick, P., Lahey, B. B., Loeber, R., Tannenbaum, L., Van Horn, Y., Christ, M. A. G., et al. (1993). Oppositional defiant disorder and conduct disorder: A meta-analytic review of factor analysis and cross-validation in a clinic sample. *Clinical Psychology Review, 13*, 319–340.

Fung, M. T., Raine, A., Loeber, R., Lynam, D. R., Steinhauer, S. R., Venables, P. H., et al. (2005). Reduced electrodermal activity in psychopathy-prone adolescents. *Journal of Abnormal Psychology, 114*, 187–196.

Gatzke-Kopp, L. M., Raine, A., Loeber, R., Stouthamer-Loeber, M., & Steinhauer, S. (2002). Serious delinquent behavior, sensation-seeking and electrodermal arousal. *Journal of Abnormal Child Psychology, 30*, 477–486.

Gordon, R. A., Lahey, B. B., Kawai, E., Loeber, R., Stouthamer-Loeber, M., & Farrington, D. P. (2004). Antisocial behavior and youth gang membership: Selection and socialization. *Criminology, 42*, 55–87.

Gordon, R. A., Rowe, H. L., Pardini, D., Loeber, R., White, H. R., & Farrington, D. P. (2014). Serious delinquency and gang participation: Combining and specializing in drug selling, theft, and violence. *Journal of Research on Adolescence, 24*, 235–251.

Hartman, C. A., Hox, J., Auerbach, J. G., Erol, N., Fonseca, A. C., Mellenbergh, G. J., et al. (1999). Syndrome dimensions of the Child Behavior Checklist and the Teacher Report Form: A critical empirical evaluation. *Journal of Child Psychology and Psychiatry, 40*, 1095–1116.

Hirschfield, P., Maschi, T., White, H. R., Goldman-Traub, L., & Loeber, R. (2006). Mental health and juvenile arrests: Criminality, criminalization, or compassion? *Criminology, 44*, 593–630.

Hoeve, M., Blokland, A., Dubas, J. S., Loeber, R., Gerris, J. R. M., & van der Laan, P. H. (2008) Trajectories of delinquency and parenting styles. *Journal of Abnormal Child Psychology, 36*, 223–235.

Hoeve, M., Smeenk, W., Loeber, R., Southamer-Loeber, M., Van der Laan, P. H., Gerris, J. R. M., et al. (2007). Long term effects of parenting and family characteristics on delinquency of male young adults. *European Journal of Criminology, 4*, 161–194.

Hoeve, M., Smeenk, W., Loeber, R., Stouthamer-Loeber, M., van der Laan, P., Gerris, J., et al. (2004). Opvoeding en delinquent gedrag bij volwassenen mannen [Child rearing and delinquency by adult men]. *Tijdschrift voor Criminologie, 46*, 347–360.

Huizinga, D., Loeber, R., Thornberry, T. P., & Cothern, L. (2000, November). Co-occurrence of serious and violent juvenile offending and other problem behaviors. *OJJDP Bulletin.*

Huizinga, D., Loeber, R., & Thornberry, T. P. (1993). Longitudinal study of delinquency, drug use, sexual activity, and pregnancy among children and youth in three cities. Public Health Reports. *Journal of the U.S. Public Health Service, 108*(1), 90–96.

Ireland, T. O., Thornberry, T. P., & Loeber, R. (2003). Violence among adolescents living in public housing: A two-site analysis. *Criminology and Public Policy, 3*, 3–38.

John, O. P., Caspi, A., Robins, R. W., Moffitt, T., & Stouthamer-Loeber, M. (1994). The "Little Five": Exploring the nomological network of the five-factor model of personality in adolescent boys. *Child Development, 65*, 160–178.

Keenan, K., Loeber, R., Zhang, Q., Stouthamer-Loeber, M., & Van Kammen, W. B. (1995). The influence of deviant peers on the development of boys' disruptive and delinquent behavior: A temporal analysis. *Development and Psychopathology, 7*, 715–726.

Keenan, K., Loeber, R., & Green, S. M. (1999). Conduct disorder in girls: A review of the literature. *Clinical Child and Family Psychology Review, 2*, 3–19.

Keijsers, L., Loeber, R., Branje, S., & Meeus, W. (2011). Bidirectional links and concurrent development of parent-child relationships and boys' offending behavior. *Journal of Abnormal Psychology, 120*, 878–889.

Keijsers, L., Loeber, R., Branje, S., & Meeus, W. (2012). Parent-child relationships of boys in different offending trajectories. A developmental perspective. *Journal of Child Psychology & Psychiatry, 53*, 1222–1232.

Kelley, B. T., Loeber, R., Keenan, K., & DeLamatre, M. (1997). Developmental pathways in boys disruptive and delinquent behavior. *OJJDP Bulletin.*

Keltner, D., Moffitt, T. E., & Stouthamer-Loeber, M. (1995). Facial expression of emotion and psychopathology in adolescent boys. *Journal of Abnormal Psychology, 104*, 644–652.

Kern, M. L., Duckworth, A. L., Urzúa, S. S., Loeber, R., Stouthamer-Loeber, M., & Lynam, D. R. (2013). Do as you're told! Facets of agreeableness and early adult outcomes for inner-city boys. *Journal of Research in Personality, 47*, 795–799.

Koolhof, R., Loeber, R., Wei, E. H., Pardini, D., & D'Escury, A. C. (2007). Inhibition deficits of serious delinquent boys with low intelligence. *Criminal Behaviour and Mental Health, 17*, 274–292.

Krueger, R. F., Caspi, A., Moffitt, T. E., White, J., & Stouthamer-Loeber, M. (1996). Delay of gratification, personality and psychopathology: Is low self-control specific to externalizing problems? *Journal of Personality, 64*, 107–129.

Lahey, B. B., Gordon, R. A., Loeber, R., Stouthamer-Loeber, M., & Farrington, D. P. (1999). Boys who join gangs: A prospective study of predictors of gang entry. *Journal of Abnormal Child Psychology, 27*, 261–276.

Lahey, B. B., Loeber, R., Waldman, I. D., & Farrington, D. P. (2006). Child socioemotional dispositions at school entry that predict adolescent delinquency and violence. *Impuls. Tidsskrift for Psykologi (Norway), 3*, 40–51.

Le Blanc, M., Loeber, R., & Janosz, M. (1999). La conduit marginale des individus, une approche dévelopemantale. *Bulletin de Psychologie, 52*, 345–354.

Lee, C., Cronley, C., White, H. R., Mun, E.-Y., Stouthamer-Loeber, M., & Loeber, R. (2012). Racial differences in the consequences of childhood maltreatment for adolescent and young adult depression, heavy drinking, and violence. *Journal of Adolescent Health, 50*, 443–449.

Loeber, R. (1990). Development and risk factors of juvenile antisocial behavior and delinquency. *Clinical Psychology Review, 10*, 1–41.

Loeber, R., & Ahonen, L. (2014). What are the policy implications of our knowledge on serious, violent, and chronic offenders? *Criminology, 13*, 117–125.

Loeber, R., DeLamatre, M., Tita, G., Cohen, J., Stouthamer-Loeber, M., & Farrington, D. P. (1999). Gun injury and mortality: The delinquent backgrounds of juvenile victims. *Violence and Victims, 14*, 339–352.

Loeber, R., Drinkwater, M., Yin, Y., Anderson, S. J., Schmidt, L. C., & Crawford, A. (2000). Stability of family interactions from ages 6 through 18. *Journal of Abnormal Child Psychology, 28*, 353–369.

Loeber, R., & Farrington, D. P. (2000). Young children who commit crime: epidemiology, developmental origins, risk factors, early interventions, and policy implications. *Development and Psychopathology, 12*, 737–762.

Loeber, R., & Farrington, D. P. (2004). Verschillende oorzaken van delinquentie tussen etnische en national groepen? Longitudinale analyses van criminaliteit onder jonge mannen in Pittsburgh and London [Are between-race and between-country causes of delinquency the same? Longitudinal analyses of young males in Pittsburgh and London]. *Tijdschrift voor Criminologie, 46*, 330–346.

Loeber, R., & Farrington, D. P. (2012). Advancing knowledge about direct protective factors that may reduce youth violence. *American Journal of Preventive Medicine, 43*, S24–S27.

Loeber, R., Farrington, D. P., Hipwell, A. E., Stepp, S., Pardini, D., & Ahonen, L. (2015). Constancy and change in the age-crime prevalence and frequency curves of offending when based on longitudinal self-reports or police charges: Comparisons by gender, race, and crime type. *Journal of Developmental and Life-Course Criminology, 1*, 150–168.

Loeber, R., Farrington, D. P., Stouthamer-Loeber, M., Moffitt, T. E., Caspi, A., & Lynam, D. (2001). Male mental health problems, psychopathy and personality traits: Key findings from the first 14 years of the Pittsburgh Youth Study. *Clinical Child and Family Psychology Review, 4*, 273–297.

Loeber, R., Farrington, D. P., Stouthamer-Loeber, M., Moffitt, T. E., & Caspi, A. (1998). The development of male offending: Key Findings from the first decade of the Pittsburgh Youth Study. *Studies on Crime and Crime Prevention, 7*, 141–172. To be republished in Kindheit und Entwicklung, Zeitschrift für Klinische Kinderpsychologie.

Loeber, R., & Hay, D. F. (1997). Key issues in the development of aggression and violence from childhood to early adulthood. *Annual Review of Psychology, 48*, 371–410.

Loeber, R., Kalb, L., & Huizinga, D. (2001, August). Serious injury victimization. *OJJDP Bulletin*.

Loeber, R., & Keenan, K. (1994). The interaction between conduct disorder and its comorbid conditions: Effects of age and gender. *Clinical Psychology Review, 14*, 497–523.

Loeber, R., Keenan, K., & Zhang, Q. (1997). Boys' experimentation and persistence in developmental pathways toward serious delinquency. *Journal of Child and Family Studies, 6*, 321–357.

Loeber, R., Menting, B., Lynam, D., Moffitt, T., Stouthamer-Loeber, M., Stallings, R., et al. (2012). Findings from the Pittsburgh Youth Study: Cognitive impulsivity and intelligence as predictors of the age-crime curve. *Journal of the American Academy of Child and Adolescent Psychiatry, 51*, 1136–1149.

Loeber, R., & Pardini, D. (2008). Neurobiology and the development of violence: Common assumptions and controversies. *Philosophical Transactions of the Royal Society B, 363*, 2491–2503.

Loeber, R., Pardini, D., Homish, D. L., Wei, E. H., Crawford, A. M., Farrington, D. P., et al. (2005). The prediction of violence and homicide in young men. *Journal of Consulting and Clinical Psychology, 73*, 1074–1088.

Loeber, R., Pardini, D. A., Stouthamer-Loeber, M., & Raine, A. (2007). Do cognitive, physiological and psycho-social risk and promotive factors predict desistance from delinquency in males? *Development and Psychopathology, 19*, 867–887.

Loeber, R., Russo, M. F., Stouthamer-Loeber, M., & Lahey, B. B. (1994). Internalizing problems and their relation to the development of disruptive behaviors in adolescence. *Journal of Research on Adolescence, 4*, 615–637. Reprinted in G. A. Adams (Ed.). (2000). *Adolescent development*: *The essential readings* (275–298). Oxford: Blackwell.

Loeber, R., & Stouthamer-Loeber, M. (1996). The development of offending. *Criminal Justice and Behavior, 23*, 12–24.

Loeber, R., & Stouthamer-Loeber, M. (1998). The development of juvenile aggression and violence. Some common misconceptions and controversies. *American Psychologist, 53*, 242–259.

Loeber, R., Stouthamer-Loeber, M., Farrington, D. P., Lahey, B. B., Keenan, K., & White, H. R. (2002). Editorial Introduction: Three Longitudinal Studies of Children's Development in Pittsburgh: The Developmental Trends Study, the Pittsburgh Youth Study, and the Pittsburgh Girls Study. *Criminal Behaviour and Mental Health, 12*, 1–23.

Loeber, R., Stouthamer-Loeber, M., Van Kammen, W. B., & Farrington, D. P. (1991). Initiation, escalation and desistance in juvenile offending and their correlates. *Journal of Criminal Law and Criminology, 82*, 36–82. Republished in S. Farrall (Ed.). (2000). *The termination of criminal careers*. Aldershot: Dartmouth (pp. 227–274).

Loeber, R., Stouthamer-Loeber, M., & White, H. R. (1999). Developmental aspects of delinquency and internalizing problems and their association with persistent juvenile substance use between ages 7 and 18. *Journal of Clinical Child Psychology, 27*, 322–332.

Loeber, R., Wei, E., Stouthamer-Loeber, M., Huizinga, D., & Thornberry, T. P. (1999). Behavioral antecedents to serious and violent juvenile offending: Joint analyses from the Denver Youth Survey, Pittsburgh Youth Study, and the Rochester Youth Development Study. *Studies on Crime and Crime Prevention, 8*, 245–263.

Loeber, R., Wei, E. H., & White, H. R. (2003). Developmental pathways to substance use and other problem behaviors. In W. L. Dewey & L. S. Harris (Eds.), *Problems of drug dependence 2002: Proceedings of the 64th Annual Scientific Meeting* (National Institute of Drug Abuse, Research Monograph Series, Vol. 183, pp. 100–101). Bethesda, MD: The College on Problems of Drug Dependence.

Loeber, R., Wung, P., Keenan, K., Giroux, B., Stouthamer-Loeber, M., Van Kammen, W. B., et al. (1993). Developmental pathways in disruptive child behavior. *Development and Psychopathology, 5*, 101–132.

Long, J. D., Loeber, R., & Farrington, D. P. (2009). Marginal and random models for longitudinal binary data with examples from criminology. *Multivariate Behavioral Research, 44*, 28–58.

Lynam, D. (1997). Pursuing the psychopath: Capturing the fledgling psychopath in a nomological net. *Journal of Abnormal Psychology, 106*, 425–438.

Lynam, R., Caspi, A., Moffitt, T. E., Loeber, R., & Stouthamer-Loeber, M. (2007). Longitudinal evidence that psychopathy scores in early adolescence predict adult psychopathy. *Journal of Abnormal Psychology, 116*, 155–165.

Lynam, D. R., Caspi, A., Moffitt, T. E., Raine, A., Loeber, R., & Stouthamer-Loeber, M. (2005). Adolescent psychopathy and the Big Five: Results from two samples. *Journal of Abnormal Child Psychology, 33*, 431–443.

Lynam, D. R., Caspi, A., Moffitt, T., Wikström, P.-O., Loeber, R., & Novak, S. (2000). The interaction between impulsivity and neighborhood context on offending: The effects of impulsivity are stronger in poorer neighborhoods. *Journal of Abnormal Psychology, 109*, 563–574.

Lynam, D. R., Derefinko, K. J., Caspi, A., Loeber, R., & Stouthamer-Loeber, M. (2007). The content validity of juvenile psychopathy: An empirical examination. *Psychological Assessment, 19*, 363–367.

Lynam, D. R., Loeber, R., & Stouthamer-Loeber, M. (2008). The stability of psychopathy from adolescence into adulthood: The search for moderators. *Criminal Justice and Behavior, 35*, 228–243.

Lynam, D., Moffitt, T., & Stouthamer-Loeber, M. (1993). Explaining the relation between IQ and delinquency: Class, race, test motivation, school failure, or self-control? *Journal of Abnormal Psychology, 102*, 187–196.

Maguin, E., & Loeber, R. (1996). How well do ratings of academic performance by mothers and their sons correspond to grades, achievement test scores, and teachers' ratings? *Journal of Behavioral Education, 6*, 405–425.

Maguin, E., Loeber, R., & LeMahieu, P. (1993). Does the relationship between poor reading and delinquency hold for different age and ethnic groups? *Journal of Emotional and Behavioral Disorders, 1*, 88–100.

Maughan, B., Rowe, R., Loeber, R., & Stouthamer-Loeber, M. (2003). Reading problems and depressed mood. *Journal of Abnormal Child Psychology, 31*, 219–229.

McBurnett, K., Lahey, B. B., Raine, A., Stouthamer-Loeber, M., Loeber, R., Kumar, A., et al. (2005). Mood and hormone responses to psychological challenge in adolescent males with conduct problems. *Biological Psychiatry, 57*, 1109–1116.

Menting, B., van Lier P. A. C., Koot, H. M., Pardini, D. A., & Loeber, R. (in press). Cognitive impulsivity and the development of delinquency from late childhood to early adulthood:

Moderating effects of parenting behavior and peer relationships. *Developmental Psychopathology*. http://www.ncbi.nlm.nih.gov/pubmed/25997462.

Messer, S. C., Angold, A., Loeber, R., Costello, E. J., Van Kammen, W. B., & Stouthamer-Loeber, M. (1995). The development of a short questionnaire for use in epidemiological studies of depression in children and adolescents: factor composition and structure across development. *International Journal of Methods in Psychiatric Research, 5*, 251–262.

Murray, J., Loeber, R., & Pardini, D. (2012). Parental criminal justice involvement and the development of youth theft, drug use, depression, and educational performance. *Criminology, 50*, 255–302.

Needleman, H. L., Reiss, J. A., Tobin, M. J., Biesecker, G. E., & Greenhouse, J. B. (1996). Bone lead levels and delinquent behavior. *Journal of the American Medical Association, 275*, 363–369.

Neumann, C. S., Hare, R. D., & Pardini, D. A. (in press). Antisociality and the construct of psychopathy: Data from across the globe. *Journal of Personality Disorders*. http://www.ncbi.nlm.nih.gov/pubmed/25181550.

Obradović, J., Pardini, D., Long, J. L., & Loeber, R. (2007). Measuring interpersonal callousness in boys from childhood to adolescence: An examination of longitudinal invariance and temporal stability. *Journal of Clinical Child and Adolescent Psychology, 36*, 276–292.

Pajer, K., Stouthamer-Loeber, M., Gardner, W., & Loeber, R. (2006). Women with antisocial behaviour: long-term health disability and help-seeking for emotional problems. *Criminal Behaviour and Mental Health, 16*, 29–42.

Pardini, D. A., Bechtold, J., Loeber, R., & White, H. (in press). Developmental trajectories of marijuana use among men: Examining linkages with criminal behavior and psychopathic features into the mid-30s. *Journal of Research in Crime and Delinquency*. http://www.ncbi.nlm.nih.gov/pubmed/25862212.

Pardini, D. A., & Fite, P. J. (2010). Symptoms of conduct disorder, oppositional defiant disorder, attention-deficit hyperactivity disorder, and callous-unemotional traits as unique predictors of psychosocial maladjustment in males: Advancing an evidence base for DSM-V. *Journal of the American Academy of Child and Adolescent Psychiatry, 49*, 1134–1144.

Pardini, D. A., Fite, P., & Burke, J. D. (2008). Bidirectional associations between parenting practices and conduct problems in boys from childhood to adolescence: The moderating effect of age and African-American ethnicity. *Journal of Abnormal Child Psychology, 36*, 647–662.

Pardini, D., & Loeber, R. (2008). Interpersonal callousness trajectories across adolescence: Early social influences and adult outcomes. *Criminal Justice and Behavior, 35*, 173–196.

Pardini, D. A., Loeber, R., Farrington, D. P., & Stouthamer-Loeber, M. (2012). Identifying direct protective factors for nonviolence. *American Journal of Preventive Medicine, 43*, S28–S40.

Pardini, D., Loeber, R., & Stouthamer-Loeber, M. (2005). Developmental shifts in parent and peer influences on boys' beliefs about delinquent behavior. *Journal of Research on Adolescence, 15*, 299–323.

Pardini, D., Obradović, J., & Loeber, R. (2006). Interpersonal callousness, hyperactivity/impulsivity, inattention, and conduct problems as precursors to delinquency persistence in boys: A comparison of three grade-based cohorts. *Journal of Clinical Child and Adolescent Psychology, 35*. 46–59.

Pardini, D. A., & Phillips, M. (2010). Neural responses to emotional and neutral facial expressions in chronically violent men. *Journal of Psychiatry and Neuroscience, 35*, 390–398.

Pardini, D. A., Raine, A., Erickson, K., & Loeber, R. (2013). Lower amygdala volume in men is associated with childhood aggression, early psychopathic traits, and future violence. *Biological Psychiatry, 75*(1), 73–80.

Pardini, D. A., White, H., Xiong, S., Bechtold, J., Chung, T., Loeber, R., et al. (2015). Unfazed or dazed and confused: Does early adolescent marijuana use cause sustained impairments in attention and academic functioning? *Journal of Abnormal Child Psychology, 43*, 1203.

Pardini, D., White, H. R., & Stouthamer-Loeber, M. (2007). Early adolescent psychopathology as a predictor of alcohol use disorders by young adulthood. *Drug and Alcohol Dependence, 88*, S38–S49.

Peeples, F., & Loeber, R. (1994). Do individual factors and neighborhood context explain ethnic differences in juvenile delinquency? *Journal of Quantitative Criminology, 10*, 141–157.

Portnoy, J., Raine, A., Chen, F. R., Pardini, D., Loeber, R., & Jennings, R. (2014). Heart rate and antisocial behavior: The mediating role of impulsive sensation seeking. *Criminology, 52*, 292–311.

Raine, A., Dodge, K., Loeber, R., Gatzke-Kopp, L., Lynam, D., Reynolds, C., et al. (2006). The Reactive-Proactive Aggression (RPQ) Questionnaire: Differential correlates of reactive and proactive aggression in adolescent boys. *Aggressive Behavior, 32*, 159–171.

Raine, A., Moffitt, T. E., Caspi, A., Loeber, R., Stouthamer-Loeber, M., & Lynam, D. (2005). Neurocognitive impairments in boys on the life-course persistent antisocial path. *Journal of Abnormal Psychology, 114*, 38–49.

Robins, R. W., John, O. P., Caspi, A., Moffitt, T. E., & Stouthamer-Loeber, M. (1996). Resilient, overcontrolled, and undercontrolled boys: Three replicable personality types. *Journal of Personality and Social Psychology, 70*, 157–171.

Russo, M. F., Loeber, R., Lahey, B., & Keenan, K. (1994). Oppositional defiant and conduct disorders: Validation of the DSM-III-R and an alternative option. *Journal of Clinical Child Psychology, 23*, 56–68.

Stepp, S. D., Pardini, D. A., Loeber, R., & Morris, N. (2011). The relation between adolescent social competence and young adult delinquency and educational attainment among at-risk youth: The mediating role of peer delinquency. *Canadian Journal of Psychiatry, 56*, 457–465.

Stouthamer-Loeber, M., Drinkwater, M., & Loeber, R. (2000). Family functioning profiles, early onset of offending, and disadvantaged neighborhoods. *International Journal of Child and Family Welfare, 4*, 247–256.

Stouthamer-Loeber, M., & Loeber, R. (2002). Lost opportunities for intervention: Undetected markers for the development of serious juvenile delinquency. *Criminal Behaviour and Mental Health, 12*, 69–82.

Stouthamer-Loeber, M., Loeber, R., Farrington, D. P., Zhang, Q., Van Kammen, W. B., & Maguin, E. (1993). The double edge of protective and risk factors for delinquency: Interrelations and developmental patterns. *Development and Psychopathology, 5*, 683–701.

Stouthamer-Loeber, M., Loeber, R., Homish, D. L., & Wei, E. (2001). Maltreatment of boys and the development of disruptive and delinquent behavior. *Development and Psychopathology, 13*, 941–955.

Stouthamer-Loeber, M., Loeber, R., Van Kammen, W. B., & Zhang, Q. (1995). Uninterrupted delinquent careers: The timing of parental help seeking and juvenile court contact. *Studies on Crime and Crime Prevention, 4*, 236–251.

Stouthamer-Loeber, M., Loeber, R., Wei, E. H., Farrington, D. P., & Wikström, P.-O. H. (2002). Risk and promotive effects in the explanation of persistent serious delinquency in boys. *Journal of Consulting and Clinical Psychology, 70*, 111–123.

Stouthamer-Loeber, M., Loeber, R., & Thomas, C. (1992). Caretakers seeking help for boys with disruptive and delinquent child behavior. *Comprehensive Mental Health Care, 2*, 159–178.

Stouthamer-Loeber, M., Van Kammen, W. B., & Loeber, R. (1992). The nuts and bolts of running a large longitudinal study. *Violence and Victims, 7*, 63–78.

Stouthamer-Loeber, M., & Wei, E. (1998). The precursors of young fatherhood and its effect on the delinquency career of teenage males. *Journal of Adolescent Health, 22*, 56–65.

Stouthamer-Loeber, M., Wei, E., Homish, D. L., & Loeber, R. (2002). Which family and demographic factors are related to both maltreatment and persistent serious delinquency? *Children's Services: Social Policy, Research, and Practice, 5*, 261–272.

Stouthamer-Loeber, M., Wei, E., Loeber, R., & Masten, A. F. (2004). Desistance from persistent serious delinquency in the transition to adulthood. *Development and Psychopathology, 16*, 897–918.

Theobald, D., Farrington, D. P., Loeber, R., Pardini, D., & Piquero, A. R. (2014). Scaling up from convictions to self-reported offending. *Criminal Behavior and Mental Health, 24*, 265.

Thompson, J., Pogue-Geile, M., Stouthamer-Loeber, M., Stallings, R., & Loeber, R. (2006). Abnormalities, psychosocial stressor exposure, and early adulthood psychotic symptoms: A prospective study. *Schizophrenia Research, 86*, S86.

Thornberry, T. P., Smith, C. A., Rivera, C., Huizinga, D., & Stouthamer-Loeber, M. (1999, September). Family disruption and delinquency, *OJJDP Bulletin*.

Thornberry, T. P., Wei, E. H., Stouthamer-Loeber, M., & Van Dyke, J. (2000, January). Teenage fatherhood and delinquent behavior. *OJJDP Bulletin*.

Vachon, D. D., Lynam, D. R., Loeber, R., & Stouthamer-Loeber, M. (2012). Generalizing the nomological network of psychopathy across populations differing on race and conviction status. *Journal of Abnormal Psychology, 121*, 263–269.

Van Domburgh, L., Loeber, R., Bezemer, D., Stallings, R., & Stouthamer-Loeber, M. (2009). Childhood predictors of desistance and level of persistence in offending in early onset offenders. *Journal of Abnormal Child Psychology, 37*, 967–980.

Van Kammen, W. B., & Loeber, R. (1992). Drugs, delinquency & discipline. *School Safety, 3*, 7.

Van Kammen, W. B., & Loeber, R. (1994). Are fluctuations in delinquent activities related the onset and offset of juvenile illegal drug use and drug dealing? *Journal of Drug Issues, 24*, 9–24.

Van Kammen, W. B., Loeber, R., & Stouthamer-Loeber, M. (1991). Substance use and its relationship to antisocial and delinquent behavior in young boys. *Journal of Youth and Adolescence, 20*, 399–414.

Van Wijk, A. P., Loeber, R., Ferwerda, H., Smulders, A., & Vermeiren, R. (2005). Jeugdige zedendelinquenten en geweldplegers. Een vergelijkende studie op grond van de Pittsburgh Youth Study [Juvenile sex offenders and violent delinquents. A comparative study based on data from the Pittsburgh Youth Study]. *Justitiële Verkenningen, 1*, 105–118.

van Wijk, A., Loeber, R., Vermeiren, R., Pardini, D., Bullens, R., & Doreleijers, T. (2005). Violent juvenile sex offenders compared with violent juvenile nonsex offenders: Explorative findings from the Pittsburgh Youth Study. *Sexual Abuse: A Journal of Research and Treatment, 17*, 333–352.

Vitacco, M. J., Neumann, C. S., & Pardini, D. A. (2014). Predicting future criminal offending in a community-based sample of males using self-reported psychopathy. *Criminal Justice and Behavior, 41*, 345–363.

Vugt, E., Loeber, R., & Pardini, D. A. (in press). Examining why young motherhood is a risk factor for persistent delinquency in boys. *Criminal Behavior and Mental Health*. http://onlinelibrary.wiley.com/doi/10.1002/cbm.1959/abstract.

Wakschlag, L. S., Pickett, K. E., Kasza, K. E., & Loeber, R. (2006). Is prenatal smoking associated with a developmental pattern of conduct problems in young boys? *Journal of the American Academy of Child and Adolescent Psychiatry, 45*, 461–467.

Wei, E. H., Loeber, R., & Stouthamer-Loeber, M. (2002). How many of the offspring born to teenage fathers are produced by repeat serious delinquents? *Criminal Behaviour and Mental Health, 12*, 83–98.

Wei, E. H., Loeber, R., & White, H. R. (2004). Teasing apart the developmental associations between alcohol and marijuana use and violence. *Journal of Contemporary Criminal Justice, 20*, 166–183.

Welsh, B. C., Loeber, R., Stouthamer-Loeber, M., Cohen, M. A., Farrington, F. P., & Stevens, B. R. (2008). The cost of juvenile crime in urban areas: A longitudinal perspective. *Youth Violence and Juvenile Justice, 6*, 3–27.

White, H. R., Fite, P., Pardini, D., Mun, E.-Y., & Loeber, R. (2013). Moderators of the dynamic link between alcohol use and aggressive behavior among adolescent males. *Journal of Abnormal Child Psychology, 41*, 211–222.

White, H. R., Jarrett, N., Valencia, E. Y., Loeber, R., & Wei, E. (2007). Stages and sequences of initiation and regular substance use in a longitudinal cohort of Black and White male adolescents. *Journal of Studies on Alcohol and Drugs, 68*, 173–181.

White, H. R., Lee, C., Mun, E.-Y., & Loeber, R. (2012). Developmental patterns of alcohol use in relation to persistence and desistance of serious violent offending among African American and Caucasian young men. *Criminology, 50*, 391–426.

White, N., & Loeber, R. (2008). Bullying and special education as predictors of serious delinquency. *Journal of Research in Crime and Delinquency, 45*, 380–397.

White, H. R., Loeber, R., Stouthamer-Loeber, M., & Farrington, D. P. (1999). Developmental associations between substance use and violence. *Development and Psychopathology, 11*, 785–803.

White, J. L., Moffitt, T. E., Caspi, A., Bartusch, D. J., Needles, D. J., & Stouthamer-Loeber, M. (1994). Measuring impulsivity and examining its relationship to delinquency. *Journal of Abnormal Psychology, 103*, 192–205.

White, H. R., Nagin, D., Repogle, E., & Stouthamer-Loeber, M. (2004). Racial differences in trajectories of cigarette use. *Drug and Alcohol Dependence, 76*, 219–227.

White, H. R., Pandina, R. J., Loeber, R., & Stouthamer-Loeber, M. (2003). Developmental patterns of drug use and crime. In W. L. Dewey & L. S. Harris (Eds.), *Problems of drug dependence 2002: Proceedings of the 64th Annual Scientific Meeting* (National Institute of Drug Abuse, Research Monograph Series, Vol. 183, pp. 107–109). Bethesda, MD: The College on Problems of Drug Dependence.

White, H. R., Shi, J., Hirschfield, P., Mun, E. Y., & Loeber, R. (2010). Effects of institutional confinement for delinquency on levels of depression and anxiety among male adolescents. *Youth Violence and Juvenile Justice, 8*, 295–313.

White, H. R., Tice, P., Loeber, R., & Stouthamer-Loeber, M. (2002). Illegal acts committed under the influence of alcohol and drugs. *Journal of Research in Crime and Delinquency, 39*, 131–152.

White, H. R., Violette, N. M., Metzger, L., & Stouthamer-Loeber, M. (2007). Adolescent risk factors for late-onset smoking among African American young men. *Nicotine & Tobacco Research, 8*, 153–161.

White, H. R., Xie, M., Thompson, W., Loeber, R., & Stouthamer-Loeber, M. (2001). Psychopathology as a predictor of adolescent drug use trajectories. *Psychology of Addictive Behaviors, 15*, 227–236.

Wikström, P.-O., & Loeber, R. (2000). Do disadvantaged neighborhoods cause well-adjusted children to become adolescent delinquents? A study of male juvenile serious offending, risk and protective factors, and neighborhood context. *Criminology, 38*, 1109–1142.

Wong, T. M. L., Loeber, R., Slotboom, A.-M., Bijleveld, C. C. J., Hipwell, A. E., Stepp, S. D., et al. (2013). Sex and age differences in the risk threshold for delinquency. *Journal of Abnormal Child Psychology, 41*, 641–652.

Youngstrom, E., Loeber, R., & Stouthamer-Loeber, M. (2000). Patterns and correlates of agreement between parent, teacher, and male adolescent ratings of externalizing and internalizing problems. *Journal of Consulting and Clinical Psychology, 68*, 1038–1050.

Zhang, Q., Loeber, R., & Stouthamer-Loeber, M. (1997). Developmental trends of delinquent attitudes and behaviors: Replication and synthesis across domains, time, and samples. *Journal of Quantitative Criminology, 13*, 181–216.

Chapters

Caspi, A., Block, J., Block, J. H., Klopp, B., Lynam, D., Moffitt, T. E., et al. (1992). A "common-language" version of the California Child Q-Sort for personality assessment. *Psychological Assessment, 4*, 512–523. Also published in M. E. Hertzig, & E. A. Farber (Eds.). (1993). *Annual progress in child psychiatry and child development* (pp. 123–149). New York: Brunner/Mazel.

Farrington, D. P. (1998). Predictors, causes and correlates of male youth violence. In M. Tonry & M. H. Moore (Eds.), *Youth violence. Crime and Justice* (Vol. 24, pp. 421–475). Chicago: Chicago University Press.

Farrington, D. P. (2001). Cross-national comparative studies in criminology. In H. N. Pontell & D. Schichor (Eds.), *Contemporary issues in crime and criminal justice: Essays in honor of Gilbert Geis* (pp. 307–320). Upper Saddle River, NJ: Prentice Hall.

Farrington, D. P., Jolliffe, D., Loeber, R., Homish, D. L., & Petechuk, D. (in press). Throwing light on the "dark figure" of crime: How many offenses do juvenile court delinquents really commit? *Office of Juvenile Justice and Delinquency Prevention Bulletin.*

Farrington, D. P., & Loeber, R. (1999). Transatlantic replicability of risk factors in the development of delinquency. In P. Cohen, C. Slomkowski, & L. N. Robins (Eds.), *Historical and geographical influences on psychopathology* (pp. 299–329). Mahwah, NJ: Lawrence Erlbaum.

Farrington, D. P., & Loeber, R. (2002). Serious and violent juvenile offenders. In M. K. Rosenheim, F. E. Zimring, D. S. Tanenhaus, & B. Dohrn (Eds.), *A century of juvenile justice* (pp. 206–236). Chicago: University of Chicago Press.

Farrington, D. P., & Loeber, R. (2013a). Causes of offending: How can they be established? In G. Bruinsma & D. Weisburd (Eds.), *Encyclopaedia of criminology and criminal justice.* New York: Springer.

Farrington, D. P., & Loeber, R. (2013b). Two approaches to developmental/life course theorizing. In F. T. Cullen & P. Wilcox (Eds.), *The Oxford handbook of criminological theory* (pp. 226–252). Oxford: Oxford University Press.

Farrington, D. P., Loeber, R., Homish, D. L., & Stallings, R. (2008). Early risk factors for homicide offenders and victims. In M. J. Delisi & P. J. Conis (Eds.), *Violent offenders: Theory, research, public policy, and practice* (pp. 79–96). Sudbury, MA: Jones and Bartlett.

Farrington, D. P., Loeber, R., Pardini, D., & Petechuk, D. (in press). Risk factors for homicide victimization among young men. *Office of Juvenile Justice and Delinquency Prevention Bulletin.*

Farrington, D. P., Loeber, R., & Stouthamer-Loeber, M. (2003). How can the relationship between race and violence be explained? In D. F. Hawkins (Ed.), *Violent crime: Assessing race and ethnic differences* (pp. 213–237). New York: Cambridge University Press.

Farrington, D. P., Loeber, R., & Ttofi, M. M. (2012). Risk and protective factors for offending. In B. C. Welsh & D. P. Farrington (Eds.), *The Oxford handbook of crime prevention* (pp. 46–69). Oxford: Oxford University Press.

Farrington, D. P., Loeber, R., & Welsh, B. C. (2013). Longitudinal-experimental studies. In D. Weisburd & A. R. Piquero (Eds.), *Handbook of quantitative criminology* (pp. 503–518). Dordrecht: Springer.

Huizinga, D., Thornberry, T. T., Knight, K. E., Lovegrove, P. J., Loeber, R., Hill, K., & Farrington, D. P. (in press). Disproportionate minority contact in the juvenile justice system: A study of differential minority contact/referral in three cities. *Office of Juvenile Justice and Delinquency Prevention Bulletin.*

Ireland, T. O., Thornberry, T. P., & Loeber, R. (2006). Residential stability among adolescents in public housing: A risk factor for delinquent and violent behavior? In J. Flint (Ed.), *Housing, urban governance and anti-social behavior: Perspectives, policy, and practice* (pp. 301–323). Bristol: The Policy Press.

Keenan, K., Stouthamer-Loeber, M., & Loeber, R. (2005). Developmental approaches to studying conduct problems in girls. In D. Pepler, C. Webster, & K. Levene (Eds.), *Development and treatment of girlhood aggression* (pp. 29–46). Hillsdale, NJ: Lawrence Erlbaum.

Lahey, B. B., & Loeber, R. (1994). Framework for a developmental model of oppositional defiant disorder and conduct disorder. In K. D. Routh (Ed.), *Disruptive behavior disorders in childhood: Essays honoring Herbert C. Quay* (pp. 139–180). New York: Plenum.

Lahey, B. B., McBurnett, K., Loeber, R., & Hart, E. L. (1995). Psychobiology of conduct disorder. In G. P. Sholevar (Ed.), *Conduct disorders in children and adolescents: Assessments and interventions* (pp. 27–44). Washington, DC: American Psychiatric Press.

Le Blanc, M., & Loeber, R. (1998). Developmental criminology updated. In M. Tonry (Ed.), *Crime and justice* (Vol. 23, pp. 115–197). Chicago: Chicago University Press.

Loeber, R. (1991). Questions and advances in the study of developmental pathways. In D. Cicchetti & S. Toth (Eds.), *Rochester symposium on developmental psychopathology: III.* Rochester, NY: Rochester University Press.

Loeber, R. (1992). Viewing emotional problems of children and adolescents from a developmental perspective. In K. Kutsah, C. Liberton, A. Algarin, & R. M. Friedman (Eds.), *5th Annual Research Conference Proceedings on a system of care for children's mental health: Expanding the research base* (pp. 53–60). Tampa, FL: Research and Training Center for Children's Mental Health.

Loeber, R. (2013a). A developmental model of delinquency. In G. Bruinsma & D. Weisburd (Eds.), *Encyclopedia of criminology and criminal justice*. New York: Springer.

Loeber, R. (2013b). Pathways to delinquency. In G. Bruinsma & D. Weisburd (Eds.), *Encyclopedia of criminology and criminal justice*. New York: Springer.

Loeber, R., & Ahonen, L. (2013). Invited address: Street killings: Prediction of homicide offenders and their victims. *Journal of Youth and Adolescence, 42*, 1640–1650.

Loeber, R., Byrd, A. L., & Farrington, D. P. (2015). Why developmental criminology is still coming of age: The influence of biological factors on within-individual change. In J. Morizot & L. Kazemian (Eds.), *Understanding the development of criminal and antisocial behavior: Theory, research and practical application* (pp. 65–74). New York: Springer.

Loeber, R., Capaldi, D. M., & Costello, E. (2013). Gender and the development of aggression, disruptive behavior, and delinquency from childhood to early adulthood. In P. H. Tolan & B. L. Leventhal (Eds.), *Disruptive behavior disorders* (pp. 137–160). New York: Springer.

Loeber, R., & Coie, J. (2001). Continuities and discontinuities of development, with particular emphasis on emotional and cognitive aspects of disruptive behavior. In J. Hill & B. Maughan (Eds.), *Conduct disorders in childhood and adolescence* (pp. 379–407). Cambridge: Cambridge University Press.

Loeber, R., DeLamatre, M., Keenan, K., & Zhang, Q. (1998). A prospective replication of developmental pathways in disruptive and delinquent behavior. In R. Cairns, L. Bergman, & J. Kagan (Eds.), *Methods and models for studying the individual* (pp. 185–215). Thousand Oaks, CA: Sage.

Loeber, R., & Farrington, D. P. (1994). Problems and solutions in longitudinal and experimental treatment studies of child psychopathology and delinquency. *Journal of Consulting & Clinical Psychology, 62*, 887–900. Republished as: Longitudinal approaches in epidemiological research on conduct problems. In F. C. Verhulst, & H. M. Koot (Eds.). (1995). *The epidemiology of child and adolescent psychopathology* (pp. 309–336). Oxford: Oxford University Press. Another version: (1997). Strategies and yields of longitudinal studies on antisocial behavior. In D. M. Stoff, J. Breiling, & J. D. Maser (Eds.), *Handbook of antisocial behavior* (pp. 125–139). New York: Wiley.

Loeber, R., & Farrington, D. P. (Eds.). (1998). *Serious and violent juvenile offenders: Risk factors and successful interventions*. Thousand Oaks, CA: Sage.

Loeber, R., & Farrington, D. P. (Eds.). (2001). *Child delinquents: Development, intervention and service needs*. Thousand Oaks, CA: Sage.

Loeber, R., & Farrington, D. P. (2008). Advancing knowledge about causes in longitudinal studies: Experimental and quasi-experimental methods. In A. Liberman (Ed.), *The long view of crime* (pp. 257–279). New York: Springer.

Loeber, R., & Farrington, D. P. (2013). The age-crime curve and its relevance for policy and interventions. In G. Bruinsma & D. Weisburd (Eds.), *Encyclopedia of criminology and criminal justice*. New York: Springer.

Loeber, R., Farrington, D. P., Stouthamer-Loeber, M., Moffitt, T. E., Caspi, A., White, H. R., et al. (2003). The development of male offending: Key findings from fourteen years of the Pittsburgh Youth Study. In T. Thornberry & M. Krohn (Eds.), *Taking stock of delinquency* (pp. 93–136). New York: Kluwer/Plenum.

Loeber, R., Farrington, D. P., Stouthamer-Loeber, M., & Van Kammen, W. B. (1998). Multiple risk factors for multi-problem boys: Co-occurrence of delinquency, substance use, attention deficit, conduct problems, physical aggression, covert behavior, depressed mood, and shy/withdrawn behavior. In R. Jessor (Ed.), *New perspectives on adolescent risk behavior* (pp. 90–149). Cambridge: Cambridge University Press.

Loeber, R., & Hay, D. F. (1994). Developmental approaches to aggression and conduct problems. In M. L. Rutter & D. H. Hay (Eds.), *Development through life: A handbook for clinicians* (pp. 488–515). Oxford: Blackwell.

Loeber, R., Keenan, K., Russo, M. F., Green, S. M., Lahey, B. B., & Thomas, C. (1998). Secondary data analyses for DSM-IV on the symptoms of oppositional defiant disorder and conduct disorder. In T. Widiger, A. Frances, H. A. Pincus, R. Ross, M. B. First, W. Davis, & M. Kline (Eds.), *DSM-IV sourcebook* (Vol. 4, pp. 465–490). Washington, DC: American Psychiatric Press.

Loeber, R., Lacourse, E., & Homish, D. L. (2005). Homicide, violence and developmental trajectories. In R. E. Tremblay, W. W. Hartup, & J. Archer (Eds.), *Developmental origins of aggression* (pp. 202–220). New York: Guilford.

Loeber, R., & Le Blanc, M. (1990). Toward a developmental criminology. In M. Tonry & N. Morris (Eds.), *Crime and justice* (Vol. 12, pp. 375–473). Chicago: University of Chicago Press. Partly republished in Le Blanc, M., & Loeber, R. Causality and the development of offending. In D. F. Hay, & A. Angold (Eds.), *Precursors, causes, and psychopathology* (pp. 233–263). Chichester: Wiley.

Loeber, R., Slot, N. W., & Stouthamer-Loeber, M. (2006). A three-dimensional, cumulative developmental model of serious delinquency. In P.-O. H. Wikström & R. Sampson (Eds.), *The explanation of crime: Contexts and mechanisms* (pp. 153–194). Cambridge: Cambridge University Press.

Loeber, R., & Stouthamer-Loeber, M. (1991). A survey of services for children with disruptive and delinquent behavior. In A. Algarin & R. M. Friedman (Eds.), *4th annual research conference proceedings on a system of care for children's mental health: Expanding the research base* (pp. 323–326). Tampa, FL: Research and Training Center for Children's Mental Health.

Loeber, R., & Stouthamer-Loeber, M. (1998). Juvenile aggression at home and at school. In D. S. Elliott, K. R. Williams, & B. Hamburg (Eds.), *Violence in American schools* (pp. 94–126). Cambridge: Cambridge University Press.

Loeber, R., Stouthamer-Loeber, M., Van Kammen, W. B., & Farrington, D. P. (1989). Development of a new measure of self-reported antisocial behavior for young children: Prevalence and reliability. In M. Klein (Ed.), *Cross-national research in self-reported crime and delinquency* (pp. 203–225). Boston: Kluwer-Nijhoff.

Loeber, R., Stouthamer-Loeber, M., Van Kammen, W. B., & Farrington, D. P. (1991). Initiation, escalation and desistance in juvenile offending and their correlates. *Journal of Criminal Law and Criminology, 82*, 36–82. Republished in S. Farrall (Ed.). (2000). *The termination of criminal careers*. Aldershot: Dartmouth (pp. 227–274).

Loeber, R., Stouthamer-Loeber, M., & Ahonen, L. (in press). Key behavioral aspects of desistance from conduct problems and delinquency. In J. Shapland, & T. Bottoms (Eds.), *Desistance from offending*. London: Routledge.

Loeber, R., Wei, E. H., & White, H. R. (2003). Developmental pathways to substance use and other problem behaviors. In W. L. Dewey & L. S. Harris (Eds.), *Problems of drug dependence 2002: Proceedings of the 64th Annual scientific meeting* (National Institute of Drug Abuse, Research monograph series, Vol. 183, pp. 100–101). Bethesda, MD: The College on Problems of Drug Dependence.

Loeber, R., White, H. R., & Burke, J. D. (2012). Developmental sequences and pathways towards serious delinquency and substance use. In T. Bliesener, A. Beelman, & M. Stemmler (Eds.), *Antisocial behavior and crime: Contributions of developmental and evaluation research to prevention and intervention* (pp. 39–52). Göttingen: Hogrefe.

Loeber, R., & Wikström, P.-O. (1993). Individual pathways to crime in different types of neighborhoods. In D. P. Farrington, R. J. Sampson, & P.-O. Wikström (Eds.), *Integrating individual and ecological aspects of crime* (pp. 169–204). Stockholm: National Council for Crime Prevention.

Lussier, P., Blokland, A., Mathesius, J., Pardini, D., & Loeber, R. (2015). The childhood risk factors of adolescent-onset and adult-onset of sex offending: Evidence from a prospective longitudinal study. In A. Blokland & P. Lussier (Eds.), *Sex offenders: A criminal career approach*. Oxford: Wiley.

Maguin, E., & Loeber, R. (1996). Academic performance and delinquency. In M. Tonry (Ed.), *Crime and justice: A review of research* (Vol. 20, pp. 145–264). Chicago: University of Chicago Press.

Moffitt, T., Caspi, A., Silva, P. A., & Stouthamer-Loeber, M. (1995). Individual differences in personality and intelligence are linked to crime: Cross-context evidence from nations, neighborhoods, genders, races, and age-cohorts. In J. Hagan (Ed.), *Current perspectives on aging and the life cycle (Vol. 4). Delinquency and disrepute in the life course* (pp. 1–34). Greenwich, CT: JAI Press.

Smith, C. A., Krohn, M. D., Lizotte, A. J., McCluskey, C. P., Stouthamer-Loeber, M., & Weiher, A. (2000). The effect of early delinquency and substance use on precocious transitions to adulthood among adolescent males. In G. L. Fox & M. L. Benson (Eds.), *Families, crime and criminal justice* (pp. 233–253). Amsterdam: JAI Press.

Stouthamer-Loeber, M. (1993). Optimizing data quality of individual and community sources in longitudinal research. In D. P. Farrington, R. J. Sampson, & P.-O. Wikström (Eds.), *Integrating individual and ecological aspects of crime* (pp. 259–277). Stockholm: National Council for Crime Prevention.

Stouthamer-Loeber, M., & Loeber, R. (2014, Fall). What we have learned from collecting data for the Pittsburgh Youth Study. Newsletter of the Division of Developmental and Life-Course Criminology.

Thornberry, T., Huizinga, D., & Loeber, R. (1995). The prevention of serious delinquency and violence: Implications from the Program of Research on the Causes and Correlates of Delinquency. In J. C. Howell, B. Krisberg, J. D. Hawkins, & J. J. Wilson (Eds.), *Sourcebook on serious, violent and chronic juvenile offenders* (pp. 213–237). Thousand Oaks, CA: Sage.

Thornberry, T. P., Huizinga, D., & Loeber, R. (2004). The causes and correlates studies: Findings and policy implications. *Journal of the Office of Juvenile Justice and Delinquency Prevention, 9*, 3–19. Reprinted in T. J. Bernard (Ed.). (2006). *Serious delinquency: An anthology* (pp. 39–52). Los Angeles, CA: Roxbury.

Tolan, P. H., & Loeber, R. (1993). Antisocial behavior. In P. Tolan & V. Cohler (Eds.), *Handbook of clinical research and practice with adolescents* (pp. 307–331). New York: Wiley & Sons.

Van Kammen, W. B., Maguin, E., & Loeber, R. (1994). Initiation into drug selling and its relationship with illicit drug use and serious delinquency. In H. J. Kerner & E. Weitekamp (Eds.), *Cross-national longitudinal research on human development and criminal behavior* (pp. 229–242). Dordrecht: Kluwer.

Van Kammen, W. B., & Stouthamer-Loeber, M. (1997). Practical aspects of data collection and data management. In L. Bickman & D. Rog (Eds.), *Handbook of applied social research methods* (pp. 375–398). Newbury Park, CA: Sage.

White, H. R., Loeber, R., & Chung, T. (in press). Racial differences in substance use: Using longitudinal data to fill gaps in knowledge. In Y. F. Thomas, & L. N. Price (Eds.), *Drug use trajectories among minority youth*. New York: Springer.

White, H. R., Pandina, R. J., Loeber, R., & Stouthamer-Loeber, M. (2003). Developmental patterns of drug use and crime. In W. L. Dewey & L. S. Harris (Eds.), *Problems of drug dependence 2002: Proceedings of the 64th Annual scientific meeting* (National Institute of Drug Abuse, Research Monograph Series, Vol. 183, pp. 107–109). Bethesda, MD: The College on Problems of Drug Dependence.

Wikström, P.-O. (1998). Communities and crime. In M. Tonry (Ed.), *The Oxford handbook of crime and punishment* (pp. 269–301). Oxford: Oxford University Press.

References

Blumstein, A., Cohen, J., Roth, J. A., & Visher, C. A. (Eds.). (1986). *Criminal careers and "career criminals", Vol. 1. Report of the Panel on Criminal Careers, National Research Council.* Washington, DC: National Academy of Sciences.

Brame, R., Bushway, S., & Paternoster, R. (2003). Examining the prevalence of criminal desistance. *Criminology, 41*, 423–448.

Brame, R., Turner, M. G., Paternoster, R., & Bushway, S. D. (2012). Cumulative prevalence of arrest from ages 8 to 23 in a national sample. *Pediatrics, 129*, 21–27.

Clarke, R. V., & Felson, M. (2011). The origins of the routine activity approach and situational crime prevention. In F. T. Cullen, C. L. Jonson, A. J. Myer, & F. Adler (Eds.), *The origins of American criminology. Advances in criminological theory* (Vol. 16, pp. 245–260). Piscataway, NJ: Transaction Publishers.

Cohen, M. A., & Piquero, A. R. (2009). New evidence on the monetary value of saving a high risk youth. *Journal of Quantitative Criminology, 25*, 25–49.

Cohen, M. A., Piquero, A. R., & Jennings, W. G. (2010a). Estimating the costs of bad outcomes for at-risk youth and the benefits of early childhood interventions to reduce them. *Criminal Justice Policy Review, 21*, 391–434.

Cohen, M., Piquero, A. R., & Jennings, W. G. (2010b). Monetary costs of gender and ethnicity disaggregated group-based offending. *American Journal of Criminal Justice, 35*, 159–172.

Cohen, M. A., Piquero, A. R., & Jennings, W. G. (2010c). Studying the costs of crime across offender trajectories. *Criminology and Public Policy, 9*, 279–305.

Eggleston, E. P., Laub, J. H., & Sampson, R. J. (2004). Methodological sensitivities to latent class analysis of long-term criminal trajectories. *Journal of Quantitative Criminology, 20*, 1–26.

Elliot, D. S., Huizinga, D., & Ageton, S. S. (1985). *Explaining delinquency and drug use*. Beverly Hills, CA: Sage.

Elliott, D. S., Huizinga, D., & Morse, B. (1987). Self-reported violent offending: A descriptive analysis of juvenile violent offenders and their offending careers. *Journal of Interpersonal Violence, 1*, 472–514.

Fabio, A., Loeber, R., Balasubramani, G. K., Roth, J., Fu, W., & Farrigton, D. P. (2006). Why some generations are more violent than others: Assessment of age, period, and cohort effects. *American Journal of Epidemiology, 164*, 151–160.

Farrington, D. P. (1973). Self-reports of deviant behaviour: Predictive and stable? *Journal of Criminal Law and Criminology, 64*, 99–110.

Farrington, D. P. (1990). Age, period, cohort, and offending. In D. M. Gottfredson & R. V. Clarke (Eds.), *Policy and theory in criminal justice: Contributions in honor of Leslie T. Wilkins*. Aldershot: Avebury.

© The Authors 2016

W.G. Jennings et al., *Offending from Childhood to Young Adulthood*,
SpringerBriefs in Criminology, DOI 10.1007/978-3-319-25966-6

Farrington, D. P. (1992). Criminal career research in the United Kingdom. *British Journal of Criminology, 32*, 521–536.

Farrington, D. P. (2002). Understanding and preventing youth crime. In *Youth justice: Critical readings*. Thousand Oaks, CA: Sage.

Farrington D.P., Jolliffe, D., Hawkins, J.D., Catalano, R.F., Hill, K.G., & Kosterman, R. (2003) Comparing delinquency careers in court records and self-reports. Criminology, 41, 933–958.

Farrington, D. P., Lambert, S., & West, D. J. (1998). Criminal careers of two generations of family members in the Cambridge Study in Delinquent Development. *Studies on Crime and Crime Prevention, 7*, 85–106.

Farrington, D. P., & Loeber, R. (1999). Transatlantic replicability of risk factors in the development of delinquency. In P. Cohen, C. Slomkowski, & L. N. Robins (Eds.), *Historical and geographical influences on psychopathology* (pp. 299–329). Mahwah, NJ: Lawrence Erlbaum.

Farrington, D. P., Loeber, R., Stouthamer-Loeber, M., Van Kammen, W. B., & Schmidt, L. (1996). Self-reported delinquency and a combined delinquency seriousness scale based on boys, mothers, and teachers: Concurrent and predictive validity for African-Americans and Caucasians. Criminology, 34, 493–517.

Farrington, D. P., Piquero, A. R., & Jennings, W. G. (2013). *Offending from childhood to late middle age: Recent results from the Cambridge Study in Delinquent Development*. New York: Springer.

Glueck, S., & Glueck, E. (1950). *Unraveling juvenile delinquency*. Cambridge, MA: Harvard University Press.

Glueck, S., & Glueck, E. (1968). *Delinquents and nondelinquents in perspective*. Cambridge, MA: Harvard University Press.

Hawkins, J. D., Kosterman, R., Catalano, R. F., Hill, K. G., & Abbott, R. D. (2005). Promoting positive adult functioning through social development intervention in childhood: long-term effects from the Seattle Social Development Project. *Archives of Pediatrics and Adolescent Medicine, 159*, 25–31.

Hindelang, M. J., Hirschi, T., & Weis, J. G. (1981). *Measuring delinquency*. Beverly Hills, CA: Sage.

Homish, D. L. (2002). Official record project manual. Unpublished manuscript, University of Pittsburgh.

Huizinga, D., & Elliott, D. S. (1986). Reassessing the reliability and validity of self-report delinquency measures. *Journal of Quantitative Criminology, 2*, 293–327.

Jennings, W. G., Maldonado-Molina, M., Piquero, A. R., Odgers, C., Bird, H., & Canino, G. (2010). Sex differences in trajectories of offending among Puerto Rican youth. *Crime and Delinquency, 56*, 327–357.

Jennings, W. G., & Reingle, J. (2012). On the number and shape of developmental/life-course violence, aggression, and delinquency trajectories: A state-of-the-art review. *Journal of Criminal Justice, 40*, 472–489.

Jolliffe, D., & Farrington, D. P. (2014). Self-reported offending: Reliability and validity. In G. J. N. Bruinsma & D. Weisburd (Eds.), *Encyclopedia of criminology and criminal justice*. New York: Springer.

Jones, B. L., Nagin, D. S., & Roeder, K. (2001). A SAS procedure based on mixture models for estimating developmental trajectories. *Sociological Methods & Research, 29*, 374–393.

Junger-Tas, J., & Marshall, I. H. (1999). The self-report methodology in crime research. In M. Tonry (Ed.), *Crime and justice* (Vol. 25, pp. 291–367). Chicago: University of Chicago Press.

Krohn, M. D., Thornberry, T. P., Gibson, C. L., & Baldwin, J. M. (2010). The development and impact of self-report measures of crime and delinquency. *Journal of Quantitative Criminology, 26*, 509–525.

Landenberger, N. A., & Lipsey, M. (2005). The positive effects of cognitive-behavioral programs for offenders: A meta-analysis of factors associated with effective treatment. *Journal of Experimental Criminology, 1*, 451–476.

Laub, J. H., & Sampson, R. J. (2003). *Shared beginnings, divergent lives: Delinquent boys to age 70*. Cambridge, MA: Harvard University Press.

Lauritsen, J. (1998). The age-crime debate: Assessing the limits of longitudinal self-report data. *Social Forces, 77*, 127–155.

Loeber, R., Farrington, D. P., Hipwell, A. E., Stepp, S., Pardini, D., & Ahonen, L. (2015). Constancy and change in the age-crime prevalence and frequency curves of offending when based on longitudinal self-reports or police charges: Comparisons by gender, race, and crime type. *Journal of Developmental and Life-Course Criminology, 1*, 150–168.

Loeber, R., Farrington, D. P., Stouthamer-Loeber, M., & White, H. (2008). *Violence and serious theft: Development and prediction from childhood to adulthood*. New York: Routledge.

Loeber, R., Farrrington, D. P., Stouthamer-Loeber, M., & Van Kammen, W. B. (1998). *Antisocial behaviour and mental health problems: Explanatory factor in childhood and adolescence*. Mahwah, NJ: Erlbaum.

Loeber, R., Wei, E., Stouthamer-Loeber, M., Huizinga, D., & Thornberry, T. P. (1999). Behavioral antecedents to serious and violent offending: Joint analyses from the Denver Youth Survey, Pittsburgh Youth Study, and the Rochester Youth Development Study. *Studies on Crime and Crime Prevention, 8*, 245–263.

Maldonado-Molina, M. M., Piquero, A. R., Jennings, W. G., Bird, H., & Canino, G. (2009). Trajectories of delinquent behaviors among Puerto Rican children and adolescents at two sites. *Journal of Research in Crime and Delinquency, 46*, 144–181.

Moffitt, T. E. (1993). Adolescence-limited and life-course-persistent antisocial behavior: A developmental taxonomy. *Psychological Review, 100*, 674–701.

Moffitt, T. E., Caspi, A., Rutter, M., & Silva, P. A. (2001). *Sex difference in antisocial behavior: Conduct disorder, delinquency, and violence in the Dunedin Longitudinal Study*. Cambridge: Cambridge University Press.

Nagin, D. S. (2005). *Group-based modeling of development*. Cambridge, MA: Harvard University Press.

Nagin, D. S. (2010). Group-based trajectory modeling: An overview. In A. R. Piquero & D. Weisburd (Eds.), *Handbook of quantitative criminology* (pp. 53–67). New York: Springer.

Nagin, D. S., & Farrington, D. P. (1992). The onset and persistence of offending. *Criminology, 30*, 301–523.

Nagin, D. S., & Land, K. C. (1993). Age, criminal careers, and population heterogeneity: Specification and estimation of a non-parametric, mixed Poisson model. *Criminology, 31*, 327–362.

Nagin, D. S., & Paternoster, R. (1991). On the relationship of past to future delinquency. *Criminology, 29*, 163–189.

Newman, O. (1972). *Defensible space: Crime prevention through urban design*. New York: Macmillan.

Osgood, D. W., Finken, L., & McMorris, B. (2002). Analyzing multiple item measures of crime and deviance II: Tobit regression analysis of transformed scores. *Journal of Quantitative Criminology, 18*, 859–866.

Piquero, A. R. (2008). Taking stock of developmental trajectories of criminal activity over the life course. In A. M. Lieberman (Ed.), *The long view of crime: A synthesis of longitudinal research* (pp. 23–78). Washington, DC: Springer.

Piquero, A. R., Brame, R., & Lynam, D. (2004). Studying career length through early adulthood among serious offenders. *Crime and Delinquency, 50*, 412–435.

Piquero, A. R., Farrington, D. P., Welsh, B. C., Tremblay, R., & Jennings, W. G. (2009). Effects of early family/parent training programs on antisocial behavior and delinquency. *Journal of Experimental Criminology, 5*, 83–120.

Piquero, A. R., Farrington, D. P., & Blumstein, A. (2003). The criminal career paradigm. In M. Tonry (Ed.), *Crime and justice* (Vol. 30). Chicago: University of Chicago press.

Piquero, A. R., Farrington, D. P., & Blumstein, A. (2007). *Key issues in criminal career research: New analyses of the Cambridge Study in Delinquent Development*. Cambridge: Cambridge University Press.

Piquero, A. R., Jennings, W. G., & Barnes, J. C. (2012). Violence in criminal careers: A review of the literature from a developmental life-course perspective. *Aggression and Violent Behavior, 17*, 171–179.

Piquero, A. R., Jennings, W. G., & Farrington, D. P. (2010). On the malleability of self-control: Theoretical and policy implications regarding a general theory of crime. *Justice Quarterly, 27*, 803–834.

Piquero, A. R., Jennings, W. G., & Farrington, D. P. (2013). The monetary costs of crime to middle adulthood: Findings from the Cambridge Study in Delinquent Development. *Journal of Research in Crime and Delinquency, 50*, 53–74.

Piquero, A. R., MacIntosh, R., & Hickman, M. (2002). The validity of a self-reported delinquency scale. *Sociological Methods and Research, 30*, 492–529.

Piquero, A. R., Schubert, C. A., & Brame, R. (2014). Comparing official and self-report records of offending across gender and race/ethnicity in a longitudinal study of serious youthful offenders. *Journal of Research in Crime and Delinquency, 51*, 525–555.

Quetelet, A. (1831). *Research on the propensity for crime at different ages* (1984th ed.). Cincinnati, OH: Anderson Publishing Company.

Shaw, C. (1930). *The Jack Roller: A delinquent boy's own story*. Chicago: University of Chicago Press.

Sherman, L. W., Gottfredson, D. C., MacKenzie, D. L., Eck, J., Reuter, P., & Bushway, S. D. (1998). *Preventing crime: What works, what doesn't, what's promising. Research in brief.* Washington, DC: National Institute of Justice.

Spelman, W. (1994). *Criminal incapacitation*. New York: Plenum.

Theobald, D., Farrington, D. P., Loeber, R., Pardini, D. A., & Piquero, A. R. (2014). Scaling up from convictions to self-reported offending. *Criminal Behaviour and Mental Health, 24*, 265–276.

Thornberry, T. P., & Krohn, M. D. (2000). The self-report method for measuring delinquency and crime. In D. Duffee (Ed.), *Criminal justice 2000* (Vol. 4, pp. 33–84). Washington, DC: US National Institute of Justice.

Tibbetts, S. G., & Piquero, A. R. (1999). The influence of gender, low birth weight, and disadvantaged environment in predicting early onset of offending: A test of Moffitt's interactional hypothesis. *Criminology, 37*, 843–878.

Wolfgang, M. E., Figlio, R. M., & Sellin, T. (1972). *Delinquency in a birth cohort*. Chicago: University of Chicago Press.

Index

© The Authors 2016

W.G. Jennings et al., *Offending from Childhood to Young Adulthood*,
SpringerBriefs in Criminology, DOI 10.1007/978-3-319-25966-6

MIX
Papier aus verantwortungsvollen Quellen
Paper from responsible sources
FSC® C105338

If you have any concerns about our products,
you can contact us on
ProductSafety@springernature.com

In case Publisher is established outside the EU,
the EU authorized representative is:
Springer Nature Customer Service Center GmbH
Europaplatz 3, 69115 Heidelberg, Germany

Printed by Libri Plureos GmbH
in Hamburg, Germany